First published in 2000
by The Pentland Press Ltd
Re-published in 2002
by the author.
This edition published by
the author, in 2009.

Written and published
by
Henry G Dobson

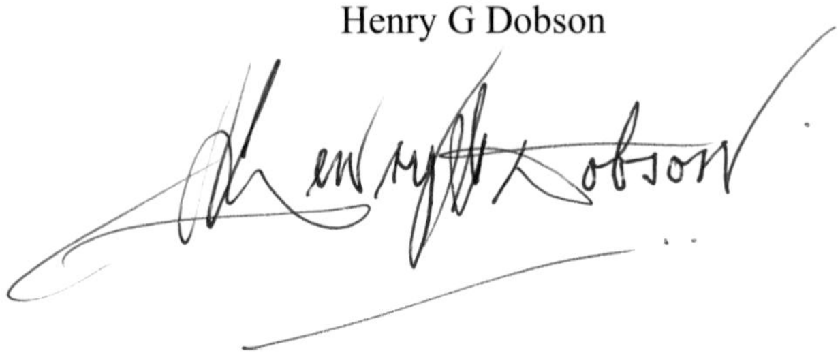

Printed and bound by Martins the Printers Ltd,
Sea View Works, Spittal,
Berwick upon Tweed.

The plate on the picture frame is inscribed as follows: "John Dobson (1878-1865). This portrait was presented to Mr Roy and Mr Ian Caller, by Ainsworth Spark Associates, Architects, and Badge Group Design, Graphic Designers, on the occasion of the opening of Linden Hall Hotel on 6th April, 1981."

The painting, which is the property of Linden Hall, shows a young man, clearly in his late twenties or early thirties, and is believed to be by J W Snow, painted in 1836. It must, therefore be a copy and not an original work, since by 1836 John Dobson was almost fifty years old – which, obviously, in this painting he is not.

Photograph featured by kind permission of Macdonald's, Linden Hall Hotel, Longhorsley, Morpeth, Northumberland, (Julia C Marshall, Manager).

Author's Note

In the first edition of 'Dobson on Dobson', published in 2000 the contents were listed in chronological order. In this edition I have listed the contents in alphabetical order – according to location: thus, Wallington Hall, for example is listed under Cambo, and Holeyn Hall under Wylam, while Mitford Hall is listed under Mitford and Belford Hall under Belford for these latter two are located in their respective villages.

While the material in this new edition is substantially the same as in the previous two I have removed some subjects where the Dobson connection might be considered somewhat tenuous and replaced them with others where the association is, shall we say, more reliable. Naturally, this also means the new edition features photographs not seen in the 2000 and 2002 editions.

I have also separated Dobson's work in the immediate area of the city (though not the suburbs) from his work elsewhere – particularly in Northumberland. There was, I admit, a temptation to include photographs of 'Dobson buildings' that no longer exist but, with very few exceptions, I have resisted this temptation.

It would have been marvellous to have included every pieces of architecture with which Dobson is associated but the logistics of such an enterprise would have incurred many difficulties, not least the tremendous expense involved: the cost of the completed volume would have been largely prohibitive. Members of the general public (for whom this present book is intended) would simply not be prepared to spend forty or fifty pounds on a single volume, whatever its merits.

To a certain extent, therefore, I share some of the frustrations of my illustrious namesake. There were numerous occasions when a lack of the necessary finance prevented him from realising his initial plans and ideas and he was obliged to resort to compromise. I would dearly have liked to write (and illustrate in full colour) a definitive work on the life and works of this remarkable individual but – for the reasons given – I must accept this is an impossible dream. So, as John Dobson came to terms with the limitations imposed upon him, I must do likewise and rejoice that within the covers of the book I have been able, once again, to draw to the attention of an interested public, a great many of the extraordinary achievements of this architectural colossus.

Introduction

I feel it is incumbent upon me at the outset to make clear I have neither architectural training nor background and therefore I may be judged unqualified to appreciate or give any kind of informed opinion on the professional merits of the work or my celebrated namesake. However, I suspect this is a deficiency I share with the great majority of my readers. But is this, I wonder, necessarily an impediment? I am under no illusion that mine is no more than simply a passionate interest in, an aesthetic appreciation of John Dobson's legacy – rather like the layman in an art gallery regarded, perhaps, by the 'cognoscenti' as an ignorant philistine unable to understand the finer techniques of a painting but who nevertheless stubbornly claims to know what he likes and who refuses to be deflected in either his taste or appreciation by the opinions of so-called 'experts'. I may well lack the essential technical knowledge necessary to confidently express an informed judgement of what is considered 'good' architecture but, like our friend in the art gallery, I also know what I like.

Even my limited comprehension of the finer points of architecture prompts me to conclude that every piece of Dobson's work cannot be deemed perfect: this would be both unrealistic and unreasonable – the man was human, after all. There were certainly occasions when he received quite justifiable criticism, and that from his peers – for some of his work at Ford and Kirknewton and on Hexham Abbey and St Nichols' Cathedral was controversial at the time.

Critics are quite rightly entitled to their opinions like everyone else but, again like many other people, I have a tendency to regard critics with the same degree of caution and scepticism I reserve for experts. So many of them, I believe, are 'little people', 'pygmies', sniping at the efforts of others whose accomplishments far outreach their own; individuals overwhelmed by an exaggerated belief in their own (imagined) importance and wont to denigrate while rarely contributing anything worthwhile themselves. Malignant criticism is worthless; qualified, constructive criticism, on the other hand, has positive value. Gervase Jackson-Stops, writing in the February 5th, 1976 edition of Country Life magazine described John Dobson as "one of the most accomplished architects ever to have practised outside London…. In no way a provincial; his work is consistently more interesting and more accomplished than many of his better known contemporaries". He was (as Lyall Wilkes described him in Tyneside Portrait) a modest and unassuming man who devoted his life wholly to architecture and the arts.

Had he decided, as a young man, to practice his 'art' in London, as many of his close friends and associates in that great city had strongly advised, there seems little doubt he would have been a nationally rather than a regionally recognised success.

Those of us fortunate to live in this unsurpassed part of the kingdom should indeed be grateful he made the decision he did for had he remained in the great metropolis then the City of Newcastle and the County of Northumberland, in particular, would, without question, have been so very much the poorer.

The more I researched the life of Dobson the more I was intrigued by the man. It would be romantic but, in truth, rather foolish to describe him as "a poor boy made good" for, frankly, this is an image far removed from reality.

His father (John Dobson Senior) was a man of substance: he owned a public house and was a landscape gardener and nurseryman on a considerable scale. Dobson's early years, therefore, were definitely not a struggle – compared to many of his contemporaries his was a comfortable existence. His parents were concerned that their son should make a success of his life and they gave him every practical support and encouragement to achieve that end.

Whatever talents he inherited from his parents, talents nourished and developed partly through their concerns and attentions and partly through the help he received from others, the fact remains he was a gifted child who, largely through his innate abilities, his perseverance and his exceptional dedication, became a gifted adult.

Not only did he become "one of the most important architects of the first half of the nineteenth century… and a very fine designer in the Classical manner and in the Gothic style, he was also a notable innovator in structural design" (Lyall Wilkes).

He was a fine water colourist. His early training as a gardener served him admirably on numerous occasions. Indeed, it was sometimes said (with more than a grain of truth) that "he almost preferred the landscape and gardens to the building itself".

Dobson-designed furniture "is as ingenious as it is striking" (Lyall Wilkes). In short, there is so much to admire and capture one's interest in the life, the work and the incredible versatility of this 'man of many parts'.

Without, as I have explained, any formal or even recognisable qualification it would have been presumptuous of me to attempt any kind of assessment or commentary on the quality of John Dobson's work: I have left that to others far more knowledgeable than I.

Instead, at the outset, I decided that my small tribute to the genius of my distinguished namesake would take the form of a photographic appreciation of the surviving works associated with this formidable character.

I confess I possess none of the expensive, sophisticated equipment so essential to the professional photographer. Photography for me, as it is for countless thousands of others, is simply a hobby, which I enjoy and which affords me (and them) a great deal of pleasure. I view the standards achieved by the professionals with deep admiration and blush at my temerity; for I am under no illusion that my unworthy efforts bear little comparison. I ask, therefore, that my modest offerings be kindly judged, but strictly within the parameters of the definition 'amateur' for I, more than my severest critic, am painfully aware of the limitations and shortcomings of my technical expertise.

My sole objective, from the very beginning, was simply to record – through the medium of photography – as many of the remaining works associated with John Dobson as I have found and photographed and that space in this book will allow. Its pages adequately illustrate, I believe, the marvellous versatility of this shy, kindly, honest and prodigious craftsman.

Sadly, over the last forty years or so, both in and around the City of Newcastle and in the neighbouring County of Northumberland particularly, much of John Dobson's work has been lost forever.

Warehouses, gaols and schools (including the Clergy Jubilee School, Carliol Square; and the Royal Jubilee School, City Road) have disappeared. Many private residences have fallen victim to the hammer, the bulldozer, the mechanical shovel and the developer's dream: Picton House, High Cross House, Jesmond Park, Jesmond Grove and Gresham Place; North Seaton Hall, Cramlington Hall, Swansfield House and West Chirton House; Sudbrooke Holme, in Lincolnshire and Oatlands House, Weybridge, in Surrey – all are no more!

His churches, too, have not escaped unscathed: St James', in Blackett Street; St Peter's, Oxford Street and the Wesleyan Church on New road – all gone. The Church of the Divine Unity and the Church of the Holy Trinity, on New Bridge Street; the Presbyterian Church on Frederick Street, South Shields; St Paul's, Hendon, Sunderland and St Mary's, Tyne Dock – none of these will ever again accommodate worshippers or be a focal point for their local communities.

Public buildings have shared the same fate: the Royal Arcade, on Pilgrim Street – described by Faulkner and Greg as "one of Dobson's most dignified compositions" – destroyed in 1963 as part of the City's 'new development'. Eldon Square has been vandalised to make way for a shopping centre: only the east side of these once fashionable terraces remains.

The Infirmary on Forth Street; the offices of the Newcastle Courant in George yard, and the Freemasons' Lodge in Middlesbrough, have all been 'erased' by various developers.

This is a truly depressing list, the more so because it is by no means complete. These are examples only of a much larger inventory of buildings John Dobson designed, built, restored or altered during a long, successful and exemplary career and even now others may well be at risk. Hopefully, most if not all of those featured here, will survive well into the twenty first century and beyond: John Dobson deserves no less.

Acknowledgements

From 1996 until 2000, as time and opportunities allowed, I photographed and often re-photographed the great majority of Dobson's surviving works in this part of England. To that end I travelled hundreds of miles throughout Northumberland, County Durham, Cleveland, part of Cumbria and, of course, the City of Newcastle and its environs, covering all four parts of the compass.

During that period it was my real privilege to meet scores of interesting people who showed me trust, great warmth and incredible help and hospitality. That so many people should have tolerated the boyish enthusiasm of a total stranger, to the extent they did, was really quite remarkable and never ceased to amaze me. That they should so readily and often eagerly show such extreme friendliness has placed me forever in their debt.

A number of them invited me into their homes: others diligently searched for papers and records or provided photographs to assist me in my researches. Almost all gave me permission to wander unsupervised through grounds and gardens 'snapping' at will. Some wrote to or telephoned third parties on my behalf: one young lady very generously placed her college thesis entirely at my disposal. All of them gave me their time and support and at all times showed, what seemed to me at least, a lively and genuine interest in my work.

When, in 2007, I decided to re-publish a revised edition of Dobson on Dobson, it quickly became apparent that a number of buildings featured in the 2000 and 2002 editions of my book had now changed ownership. As a matter of courtesy it was necessary, therefore, to contact their new owners and obtain permission to publish photographs of their properties. This I did and, with only one or two exceptions they were happy that I should do so. Indeed, I was overwhelmed yet again by the measure of interest, kindness and support I had received previously.

It would, alas, be impossible to acknowledge in print every person who, in some small way or other, contributed to the success of 'Dobson...' Nevertheless, it is only right and proper that I should readily and happily mention those who gave me permission to photograph their properties. As for the others – whether they work in shops or offices, schools or libraries; whether they live in fine houses, castles or lodges, rectories or old vicarages – they will know who they are and that I am immensely indebted to them for their patience, goodwill and inestimable kindness; thank you all so very much.

Lilburn Tower (Alnwick): Mr Duncan Davidson. Belford Hall (Belford): Belford Hall Management Company Ltd. Belsay Hall (Belsay): English Heritage.

St Cuthbert's Vicarage (Benfieldside): Reverend Martin Jackson. Benwell Tower (Benwell): the BBC. Wynyard Park (Billingham): Cameron Hall Developments Ltd, Sir John and Lady Hall. Blagdon Hall (Blagdon, Seaton Burn): The Hon. Matthew White Ridley. Axwell Park (Blaydon): D.A.R.E. (Northern) Ltd, Bolam Hall and Lake (Bolam): Professor Gordon R Dickson and Mrs D Ballinger. Gibside (Burnopfield): the National Trust. Wallington Hall (Cambo): the National Trust. Doxford Hall (Chathill): Mr Brian and Mrs Shirley Burnie. The Old Vicarage (Longstone House): Dr Sebastian and Mrs Rebecca Moss (East Wing); Mr Michael and Ms Alison McManus (West Wing). Lambton Castle (Chester-le-Street): Mr Robert Kirton-Darling, Estate Manager. Chollerton Grange (Chollerton): 'the owner'. Fallodon Hall (Christon Bank): Mr P O R Bridgeman. Craster Tower (Craster): Mrs J M Craster and Miss M D Cra'ster. Arcot Hall (Dudley): the Committee and Secretary of Arcot Hall Golf Club. Embleton Tower (Embleton):Mr K J Seymour-Walker. Newton Villa Farm (Felton): Mr and Mrs David N O Scott. Acton House (Felton): Mr A and Mrs E Ferguson. Sheriff Hill Hall (Gateshead Fell): Gateshead Central Library. Shawdon Hall (Glanton): Mr R F H Cowen. Glanton Pyke (Glanton): Mr and Mrs J S R Swanson. Bellister Castle and Tower House (Haltwhistle): the National Trust. The Old Vicarage (Haltwhistle): Mr Colin Creighton. Unthank Hall (Haltwhistle): Mr and Mrs W R Webster. Harbottle Castle House (Harbottle): Mrs M B Wilson. Angerton Hall (Hartburn): Mr and Mrs T E Stephens. Meldon Park (Hartburn): Mr James Cookson. The Old Vicarage (Hartburn): Mr J and Mrs M Smart. Hawthorn Tower (Hawthorn): Easington District Council. Beaufront Castle (Hexham): Mr J Aidan Cuthbert.. Hackwood House (Hexham): Mr and Mrs R W Wassell. The Hermitage (Hexham): Mrs Veronica Allgood and the Trustees of Miss J E Allgood. Hexham House (Hexham): Tynedale Council. The Leazes (Hexham): The Leazes Management Company; Dr Thomas W Graham, Secretary, Sandhoe House (Hexham): Mr J Aidan Cuthbert. Welton Keeper's Cottage and Whittle Dean Reservoirs (Horsley-on the Hill): Northumbria Water. Haughton Castle (Humshaugh): 'the owner'. Jesmond Dene House (formerly Black Dene House) (Jesmond): Jesmond Dene House Ltd, Mr Eric Kortenbach, General Manager. Jesmond Towers (formerly La Sagesse High School) (Jesmond): the Daughters of Wisdom. Nazareth House (formerly Sandyford Park and Villa Reale), now the Lower School of Central Newcastle High School (Jesmond): Mrs H T French, (Headteacher). Minsteracres Monastery (Kiln Pit Hill): Father Luke Mcgee. Burnhopeside Hall (Lanchester): Mrs Christine Hewitt. Longhirst Hall (Longhirst): Mr Stephen Cowell; Mrs Lesley Williamson, General Manager. Linden Hall (Longhorsley): Macdoanld's; Julia C Marshall, Manager. Mitford Hall (Mitford): Mr B S Shepherd. The Chantry (Morpeth): Dawn Goodwill-Evans; CMBC Tourism Officer. Nunnykirk School (Netherwitton) Mr S Dalby-Ball, Headmaster. Newbrough Hall (Newbrough): Mr Mark Henry Beaumont. The Castle Keep (Newcastle upon Tyne): The Society of Antiquaries.

The Market Keeper's House (Newcastle): Tyne and Wear Development Corporation. Portland House (formerly the Lying-in-Hospital) (Newcastle): The Newcastle Building Society. The Riding School (Newcastle): University of Northumbria; Professor Gilbert Smith, Vice-Chancellor. The Archbold and Williamson Monuments (St Nicholas' Cathedral, Newcastle): Mr R Cunliffe, Verger (1997). Trinity House (Newcastle): The Brethren of Trinity House, Captain Rennison Shipley. The Watergate Building (Newcastle): Home Group Ltd, Mrs Brenda Williamson. Mowden Hall School (formerly Newton Hall) (Newton): Mr Ben Beardmore-Gray Headmaster). North Seaton Hall (North Seaton): Wansbeck District Council. Prestwick Lodge (Prestwick Village): Mr and Mrs Michael Wilson. Rock Hall (Rock): Mr C J Bosanquet. The Navigational Beacons (Guile Point, Ross Sands): Trinity House, Captain Rennison Shipley. Hamsterley Hall (Rowlands Gill): Mr Tom Gibson. Seaton Delaval Hall (Seaton Delaval): The late Lord Hastings. Holy Trinity Vicarage (Seghill): Mr C Lawson. Flotterton House (Snitter): Mr James Walton. Cheeseburn Grange (Stamfordham): Mr S F Riddell, Trewhitt Hall (Thropton): Mrs Elizabeth R Nicholl. The Percy Chapel (Tynemouth Priory): English Heritage. Chipchase Castle (Wark-on-Tyne): Mr and Mrs P Torday. Holme Eden Hall (Warwick Bridge): Cumbrian Homes; Mr N A Pallister. Holme Eden Vicarage (Warwick Bridge): Reverend J Stuart Casson. Bolton Hall (West Bolton): Mr and Mrs J Hylton-Young. Thirston House (West Thirston): Mr and Mrs Brian Reed. Holeyn Hall (Wylam): Dr John and Mrs Shirley Williams and Mrs Ann Brough. Bradley Hall (Wylam): Mr and Mrs R M C Simpson.

Special thanks to my wife, Susan, and to Mr Ron Hodgson, Ms Pat Hughes and Mr Bob Huggins, for their invaluable technical expertise and assistance: my grateful thanks to each and every one of you.

John Dobson was born, the second of twelve children, to John and Margaret (nee Clark) Dobson, on December 9th, 1787, in Chirton, North Shields. At a very early age he showed a propensity for drawing and amusing stories are told of the wrath of the villagers on finding their gates and shutters decorated with sketches in chalk, by his furtive hand. Mr Lawson the village schoolmaster perceiving his bent, gave him a set of drawing materials whereupon the lad ceased his 'al fresco' efforts. He must have advanced quickly in skill as he was, while still a child, appointed to the office of 'Honorary Draftsman' to a Mr McClashan, a celebrated damask weaver in the neighbourhood. At the age of only eleven or twelve he actually developed designs which were to be of valuable assistance to Mr McClashan in his trade.

John's father, who appears to have been a man of both uncanny perception as well as considerable ability, wisely determined to give his son the advantage of a thoroughly good English education and granted young John every facility to pursue his studies after leaving the care of Mr Lawson.

At the age of fifteen John was placed by his father as a pupil with Mr David Stephenson who was, at that time, Newcastle's leading builder/architect. In this office John made rapid progress and gained not only a thorough knowledge of architecture but 'an unusual acquaintance' with carpentry and masonry. During this period he also studied surveying with a Mr Hall of Stamfordham.

In these aesthetic days some might consider this practical training beneath the dignity of the profession. However, the bitter experience of the eminent French architect, Violett le Duc, would seem to suggest otherwise. Monsieur le Duc tells us that for two years he was set to copy drawings of buildings of which he knew absolutely nothing, neither their age, their purpose nor their location. He then worked in an architect's office, tracing plans and nothing else, except occasionally being told to make some detailed drawings – but not knowing how – and never seeing the smallest part of a building executed.

During the time Dobson worked under the supervision of David Stephenson he also spent time with Boniface Moss, an Italian refugee, by whom he was instructed in the arts of fencing, perspective and enamel painting. In 1810 John Dobson completed his apprenticeship and Stephenson strongly advised him to establish himself in Newcastle strictly as an architect. Before commencing his chosen profession, however, John took himself off to London to seek instruction from John Varley, "the father of English water-colour drawing".

Initially Varley was extremely reluctant to accept any new pupil, declaring he could not spare even half an hour of his valuable time. But, observing the look of intense disappointment on the face of young Dobson, he eventually relented and consented to give him lessons at five in the morning, his time during the rest of the day being fully occupied.

Varley quickly recognised the uncommon qualities of his pupil and not only agreed to give him daily lessons but invited him to lodge at his house until alternative accommodation could be arranged. A mutual esteem between master and pupil was rapidly established which was to last long after Dobson returned from London.

During his first visit to the capital John Dobson formed numerous other lasting relationships, with various eminent men, one of whom – Sydney Smirke – was to become his future son-in-law. Smirke, and others, strongly urged him to establish himself as an architect in London where, very likely, career prospects and opportunities would have presented themselves very readily. However, we are told by his daughter, Margaret Jane (in her father's biography) that Mr Dobson "had a retiring nature and he shrank from what appeared too great an enterprise for one so young". On the other hand, it may have been that a more astute Mr Dobson realised that aspiring young architects in the great metropolis were 'two-a-penny' and consequently competition would be extremely fierce, whereas back home, in his native north-east, they were very 'thin on the ground'. Better, perhaps, to be a big fish…. Though we can never know his real motives let us exercise a little charity and, setting cynicism aside, let us assume it was, as his daughter suggests, for reasons of modesty.

On his return to the north Dobson was quickly acquainted with reality; in short, that "it is easier to profess an art than to practise it". Despite the fact that the only two professional architects to be found between York and Edinburgh were himself and Ignatius Bonomi, as a young man newly qualified and relatively unknown, and at the start of his career, he soon discovered that the demand for his services had to be created. Commissions came slowly at first but he never allowed himself to be idle for want of work. During periods of unemployment he travelled throughout England and France, studying and sketching various forms of architecture, a habit he continued all his life. In 1816 at the age of twenty-nine, he married Isabella Rutherford of Gateshead (the eldest daughter of Alexander Rutherford), a lady of not inconsiderable artistic talent. During almost thirty years of marriage John Dobson fathered eight children though, sadly, only four survived into adulthood. The eldest son, John Junior, assisted his father for some years in his office on Pilgrim Street but became a Master Mariner and showed little interest in following in his father's footsteps. The youngest son, Alexander Ralph, inherited all his father's artistic genius and had a brilliant future ahead of him.

Unfortunately the fates conspired to prevent this and he met a cruel and untimely death in an explosion that occurred in Gateshead, on October 4th 1854.

It was said that John Dobson never really recovered from the tragic loss of Alexander although he continued working until 1862 when he suffered a severe stroke: this effectively brought to an end his extraordinary working life.

His surviving daughters were Isabella and Margaret Jane. Isabella married Sydney Smirke R.A., with whom his father-in-law shared many interests. They remained close friends and colleagues throughout the remainder of Dobson's life and regularly consulted each other professionally – comparing notes and exchanging sketches. Unhappily, and like so many of Dobson's papers, the great majority of these correspondences – so full of interest from an architectural point of view – are lost forever.

In 1885, Margaret Jane published her Memoir – a biography of her father, John. I have referred to this extensively in my Profile and I make no apology for doing so since there is not, to my knowledge, a more accurate, informed, colourful or more detailed account of the life of John Dobson to be found anywhere. Her critics (and they are legion) have claimed that the same degree of accuracy does not always extend to the list of her father's works: this cannot be denied but is a separate issue. Margaret Jane clearly held her father in the highest regard and her book is written with obvious pleasure and a justifiable pride in his many achievements, for John Dobson was indeed a remarkable man, arguably the greatest architect this region of England has ever produced in any age. Her closing description of her much loved and revered parent is tinged with a certain sympathy and regret that, in his lifetime at least, his genius was not always as widely recognised as she felt it ought to have been.

She wrote – The man of productive genius can only be known through his works and this, which is true of all, is especially true of the architect. His works, unlike those of the painter or the musician, are to be found at great distances from one another and only figured representation of them can be brought together. He matures his designs in the privacy of his home and when they are put in execution, we can see the joiner and the mason at work, not the architect.

The characteristics of great architects are less known; their names are more easily forgotten than any other of the tribe of artists. The designers of many of the noblest buildings of the world have been lost to fame. It may be added that the architect is more liable to disappointments from baffled enterprise than those engaged in any other profession.

He has to contend with the wills and prejudice of others; he is hampered by committees, and the designs by which he is expected to become famous are either cut down for want of means or, perhaps, altogether abandoned. Mr Dobson had many such trials to overcome, but his elevated love of his art never failed to surmount all depressing incidents.

Margaret Jane concluded her Memoir with the following heartfelt tribute….. Few men ever spent so long a life in so laborious a manner, having gained the love and esteem of all who knew him. It would be difficult to over-praise his generous, genial, simple, warm-hearted, honourable nature.

In 1859 he became the first President of the Northern Architectural Association. He died, at his home in New Bridge Street, in the heart of the city he loved so well, on the 8th of January, 1865.

John Dobson is buried in Newcastle General Cemetery, Jesmond, together with his wife, Isabella, who predeceased him by some twenty years.

Part One

Northumberland

-------- and beyond.

The present church dates from the end of the 14th century but it has been restored several times, most notably in 1464, "which endowed it with some of the finest architecture in the North of England". (Purves) Re-ordering by the Adams brothers (Robert and James), in 1782, produced a very ornate interior.

By the beginning of the 19th century it had become apparent that there was a need to increase the seating capacity in the church. There had been for some time something of a religious revival in the town and the seating provision for these increasing attendances at the church was clearly inadequate for the size of the congregation.

At that time (1811) there were several small galleries in the church: one at the west end (the Foster gallery, dating from the early 18th century); the Brown and Latin galleries, on the north side of the building (the first for family use, the other owned by Alnwick Corporation, for pupils attending the Latin school) and Grey's gallery, on the south side.

In 1818 a faculty was granted by the Bishop of Durham empowering the churchwardens to clear away the whole of the box-pews and galleries in the nave and aisles. The entire church was to be re-seated with new pews and a fund was started to build a large gallery at the west end of the church.

This gallery was the principal part of the alterations made by John Dobson in response to the request for more seating made by the churchwardens and the "Four and Twenty". The total cost of the work amounted to £2,189.0.10¼d; £1018.8.1d was raised from the sale of seats; the Duke donated £300 and church rates raised a further £871.0.9¼d.

Dobson's gallery was supported on fourteen iron pillars and in order that the congregation assembled in the gallery could see into the main body of the church alternate pillars were removed from the north and south nave and the arches rounded off. Two massive tie-beams were built into the stonework above the north colonnade, between the west outer wall and the chancel arch so that the pressure of the semi-circular outer arches would not push the west wall out of the vertical. The west arch in the north aisle was blocked off to further strengthen the wall.

The main access to the gallery was by a staircase on the west side of the church. There were two more sets of stairs on the north and south sides where the gallery joined the church walls.

All of this was the work of John Dobson.

Twenty years later the gallery had to be enlarged because its capacity (of almost three hundred) was by then considered inadequate.

In 1863, however, Anthony Salvin refurbished the church and the gallery was completely removed. The four pillars which had been taken out when the gallery was built were replaced and the arches were restored to their former Decorated style – "returning (the church) to a style believed to be more in keeping with its origin".

Lilburn Tower   (near Alnwick)

Designed in 1828, for Henry Collingwood, to replace an earlier house, it is, in all respects, 'except its architectural style', a perfect example of an 1820s house.

The entrance front would have been perfectly symmetrical had Dobson's design remained unaltered but his plan had to be modified.

The porte-cochère was subsequently moved from a position between the projecting wings to the position it occupies now. This was done, sometime between 1840-50, we are given to understand, to prevent draughts from outside finding their way into the main hall.

Gervase Jackson-Stops, writing in the November 8th, 1973, edition of Country Life, said "Dobson's dexterity in translating Greek into Tudor must be admired, for the result is completely successful".

The extra cost involved in departing from the straight lines and simplicity of the classical design into the realms of the picturesque is shown in the fact that the cost of Meldon Park (1832) was £7,188.1.11 (excluding the stables), while the cost of the towers and turrets at Lilburn (four years earlier, in 1828) was £21,975 (also excluding the stables).

John Grundy and Grace McCombie have made the following observation: Dobson was equally happy to design in the Gothic style, though the results are not so unreservedly successful. His best Gothic buildings are substantial country houses. Lilburn Tower, built in the middle of his finest Grecian period is, in reality a symmetrical classical design, 'wrapped in Tudor-Gothic veneer'.

It is a beautiful house, nevertheless; wonderfully sited (as almost all of Dobson's houses were) and with a fine and complete set of his own decorations and furnishings.

Lilburn Tower is on a site of great natural beauty. It stands on a wide terrace with views across the Till and Lil Burns, on the east and south respectively. It has fine gardens and a magnificent approach road lined by trees for almost a mile.

Originally, the entrance front like the south elevation was perfectly symmetrical but, in 1843, E J Collingwood recalled the architect, John Dobson, and the magnificent porte-cochère which, hitherto had been situated in the centre of the entrance front, between the projecting wings, had to be moved slightly north, to the left as you face the entrance – "to prevent draughts from outside finding their way into the main hall".

At this time the great staircase was separated off from the hall.

The symmetrical south front with its towers and turrets and mullioned windows.

The east front.

Abraham Dixon bought the village of Belford in 1726, for £12,000. The farming was backward and the 'town' had improved little since 1636, when it was described as "the most miserable, beggarly, sodden town, or town of sodes, that ever was made in an afternoon of loam and sticks. In all the town not a loaf of bread, not a quart of beer, nor a lock of hay, nor a peck of oats, and little shelter for horse or man". Abraham Junior succeeded his father, in 1743, but gave up trade to devote time to improving his estate, which he did very successfully, planting hedges and plantations, digging ditches, establishing farms: he built a tannery and a woollen factory: he mined coal and built an inn, with accommodation for travellers. Had he lived today no doubt he would be described as an 'entrepreneur'.

Dixon left the old manor house and in its place he built a new house to designs by James Paine, which was completed in 1756.

The main façade to the hall, facing south, is five bays wide and has a 'piano nobile'. The central Ionic portico, with four half-columns, is flanked by slightly recessed Ionic pilasters. The entablature then breaks back over the outside windows, only to be brought forward again by twin Ionic pilasters which frame the façade. The side elevations are much simplified versions of the front with the architectural detail reduced to a skeleton. The slight projection of the portico is retained but the pilasters, entablature and pediment have gone and so have the balusters.

Abraham Dixon died in 1782 and left Belford to his great nephew, Arthur Onslow (later Lord Onslow) who later sold it, in 1810, to a Newcastle merchant, William Clarke, who called in John Dobson to 're-order' the house. Dobson condemned James Paine for the manner in which the front door opened directly into the hall, thus ensuring the house was always cold, together with Paine's habit of placing the hall in the middle of the south front, taking up the best view.

Dobson complained that by making his entrance on the side where the best aspect is usually obtained Paine had prevented the ground from being properly planted, so as to afford the necessary shelter, and deprived the building of the advantage of rich and fully dressed ground about the house.

It was not often Dobson was given to angry criticism and his opinion of Paine verged on the contemptuous. Paine, he reproved, was unfortunately considered a great authority (on the building of houses): "We thus see," admonished Dobson, "how much mischief an incompetent man may do, if he be but favoured by fortune and fashion: not only do his patrons suffer but an example is set by which mischief is perpetuated".

Belford Hall: a large stone mansion, designed by James Paine and altered and enlarged by John Dobson in 1817-18.

In 1818, to overcome the problem of cold air entering the hall, John Dobson tuned Belford 'back to front', making a new entrance on the north side, with an Ionic porch entering into a top-lit, single-storey hall. This then led into the staircase hall. Dobson also remodelled Paine's three-sided staircase as well as adding large wings on either side of the house. On the south side these were kept very simple, with detail taken from Paine, but the composition of the north front was deliberately picturesque. Belford Hall: Dobson's new entrance on the north side.

The single-storeyed South Lodge (also designed by Dobson) has a very plain portico, supported by four, square pillars.

The Parish Church of St Mary   (Belford)

It isn't known when the first church was built in Belford but there was one in 1100 – probably a wooden building served by the monks of Lindisfarne. The first stone church was built in Norman times, around 1200. In 1615 the church was entirely rebuilt and was a plain, rectangular design with a door at the west end of the south side and a bell turret; the date 1615 is carved over the door nearer the east end.

Due to the poor state of repair, an extensive restoration programme was carried out in 1700.

The restoration of the chancel, by John Dobson, was started in 1828 and in 1829 the present building was built.

As the old building was unable to accommodate the population, the north aisle was added and a gallery above the north and west aisles was constructed. The bell turret was replaced by a tower surmounted by four pinnacles. It is thought that during this rebuilding programme the private chapel was incorporated into the church, to become the chancel. The most interesting feature of the chancel (apart from the Norman arch) is the small south window, which is the one original window left untouched in the church. It has since been filled with glass designed by Harold Easton.

The clock was installed in the tower, in 1841: the porch was added in 1844 – great complaints having been made in Winter about the cold in that part of the church.

The porch cannot have been an unqualified success for we are told "… the congregation continued to shiver until 1854 when gas stoves were purchased". The pulpit was replaced in 1860 and the old 'box pews' were removed in 1879 and replaced with those we see today.

During the course of John Dobson's restoration and rebuilding programme, in 1828-29, the Norman chancel arch was plastered over and forgotten about until some fifty years later when it was found again, its zigzag mouldings still intact.

In 1829 Dobson rebuilt the nave and added a north aisle and the west tower.

*I am obliged to the Reverend Adrian J Hughes, Vicar of St Mary's, for his kind permission to use extracts from the church notes (June, 1998).

Belsay Hall is, along with the Moot Hall of John Stokoe (1756-1836), one of the two outstanding monuments of Greek Revival architecture in the north-east. Indeed, in terms of architectural quality, originality and craftsmanship, it is by far the finer of the two.

It seems to have been entirely the conception of its owner, Sir Charles Monck (1779-1867) of Belsay Castle, though designed with the advice and aid of Sir William Gell (1777-1836) and, perhaps, the young John Dobson. It was begun in 1807 but not ready for living in until 1817.

The plan is a square with sides of six bays: two sides are very plain with four of the most delicate Doric pilasters separating large windows which punctuate the walls without any mouldings.

The entrance side is divided into three equal parts by these pilasters the central portion is set back behind two giant Doric fluted columns 'in antis' – ie flush with the line of the wall.

The house is raised like an actual Greek Temple on a podium of three steps and topped by a heavy triglyph frieze and cornice.

The house… expresses all the qualities of Greek architecture – simplicity, purity and grandeur without descending to the mere copying of temple facades.

The masonry work is of exceptionally high quality (the original drawings are dimensioned n decimals to .001 of an inch) from stone quarried on the site.

Bruce Allsopp and Ursula Clark (Historic Architecture of Northumberland and Newcastle upon Tyne) describe the south front of the Hall as 'a massive and reasonably correct Greek cornice surmounting a curiously improved design'.

There are claims that a young John Dobson may have had some small part in the design of the Hall – that he made a contribution to the drawing up of the plans. Allsopp and Clark write that he possibly made the original drawings for the Ionic capitals in the atrium but the columns are an original invention for which there is no Greek precedent.

Andrew Greg believes that any connection between Dobson and Belsay Hall is purely circumstantial and that any Dobson involvement has never been proved. Lyall Wilkes, on the other hand, tells us that 'from some uncertain date' Dobson assisted Sir Charles in the design of parts of Belsay Hall. To substantiate his claim Wilkes refers us to extracts from a notebook belonging to Sir Stephen Middleton (N.C.R.O. ZMI/S53): "Sir Charles had difficulty in getting the Ionic capitals cut from the drawings: Dobson, the architect, modelled one in clay or made a plaster cast for the masons to work from. Dobson also drew the capitals of the Doric columns in the Portico; the curve is a hyperbola".

27

This lovely little church, near Shotley Bridge (County Durham), in the Early English style, is by John Dobson (1849-50).

The Tower has a 'broach spire', like that on another of Dobson's churches, St Cuthbert's on Bensham Road, Gateshead.

The Newcastle Journal of 11th January 1851, claims that John Dobson built the Vicarage around the time he also built the church. The Vicar, the Reverend Martin Jackson, also believes that 'on the grounds of proximity and style' his is a Dobson building.

Photographed by kind permission of Reverend Jackson.

'The imposing castellated building', says Tomlinson, 'stands on the site of an old tower which belonged to the Priors of Tynemouth and was their summer residence. Added to the tower was a small domestic chapel (below right) and burying ground wherein internments took place, until 1759.

The square, castellated Tudor mansion was rebuilt by John Dobson in 1830-31, for Thomas Crawhall.

Designed by John Dobson in 1831-2 and built by Richard Grainger, who is buried in the grounds of the church.

This, claims Pevsner, was Dobson's first venture into the Norman style. Faulkner and Greg write that "the church, however Georgian in plan, was quasi-medieval in effect. St James' has undecorated arches and... was still rather classical in feel".

Plans survive indicating a 'rectangular scheme', with neither aisles nor chancel and with a centrally placed tower (without a spire), providing the west entrance to the church.

The ground floor was totally occupied by seating: there are galleries to the west and the north and south sides of the nave are partially galleried.

There have been numerous additions to the church since 1832: vestries were added in 1879-80; the spire, choir vestry and porch in 1895 and the north aisle in 1902.

Described by J M Robinson as "probably County Durham's nearest equivalent to a grand stately home".

The entrance front (facing north) is a version of the Waterloo Palace design with the same rectangular, balustraded silhouette, pedimented portico, slightly emphasised end-bays, and a full-height central hall, expressed as a dome on the exterior.

Thirteen windows wide with a heavy hexastyle, giant, Corinthian portico (or porte-cochère) two columns deep.

At each end, on the ground floor, there is a tripartite window.

John Dobson was employed by Lord Londonderry in 1832 and, again, according to accounts in the Durham County Records Office, in 1838. Neville Whittaker (The Old Halls and Manor Houses of Durham) states that the Marquis again employed Dobson in 1845, to carry out some of the necessary repairs and restoration after the fire in 1841.

The south front, facing the lake, is the original 18th century house belonging to the Tempests.... a rich, coal-owning family. In 1819, Lady Jane Vane-Tempest married Lord Stewart (who later became the Marquis of Londonderry) and it was the Marquis who decided to 'rebuild on palatial lines'.

The garden front (the west elevation) has bowed pavilions at either end, but it is otherwise relatively plain.

The foundation stone was laid in 1822 and the work was almost completed when, in 1841, a disastrous fire broke out. The repairs and restoration, it is said, cost just less than half the original cost of more than £100,000.

The west face of the church is heavily buttressed.
It also has five stepped Lancet windows – three of them 'blind'.
The church is topped by a corbelled bellcote.

St Joseph's was designed by John Dobson and built between 1842-44.

36

"The Newcastle Courant" of May the 20th, 1842, records that John Dobson built the Church of St Joseph, the school (now demolished!) and the presbytery, attached, in the Gothic style.

In 1848-49, John Dobson added north and south transepts, to increase seating capacity, to the former Parish Church of St Michael's... a fact confirmed by the Newcastle Daily Chronicle of July 6th, 1849.

St Michael's is now Sunderland Minster.

Further alterations took place in 1872, 1874 and 1887.

The Gothic tower is believed to be of 1807.

The south front.

The east front.

Blagdon Hall was built by Matthew White, a Newcastle merchant, between 1735-40 and incorporated a little of its 17th century predecessor.

Further additions were made in 1826 and 1830.

The rather plain north wing, partly by John Dobson, was added c.1820.

The south front has two-and-a-half-storeys and seven bays: it is distinguished by a central, three-bay pediment. The first floor windows are all pedimented with coats-of – arms and garlands.

To the left of the Hall is a single-storey, three-bay addition of c.1820.

The east front is also seven bays wide and still shows traces of its 18th century pilasters. The central doorway is by Robert Lutyens (1948-9)

The north wing.

Axwell Park is an unusually large Palladian villa, built by James Paine, for the eminent politician Sir Thomas Clavering, in 1758.

The Claverings were established at Axwell during the reign of Elizabeth the First and their old mansion, White House, stood half a mile west of the present house.

The Hall and surrounding parkland was passed down through the Clavering family for a hundred and sixty years but in 1920 the family fortune collapsed and Maria Margaret Napier-Clavering sold the Hall.

In 1922 it became the Newcastle Ragged and Industrial School., creating a centre for boys ' on the verge of crime'. Part of the building became the Headmaster's house, while a workshop and kitchen were added for the one hundred and fifty boys. In 1981 (because of the falling pupil numbers) the school transferred to the smaller Clavering House, within the grounds. Five years later, in 1986, the Hall was sold to a private company with a view to its restoration: sadly, this didn't happen.

When these photographs of Axwell Park were taken, in June 1998, the house was in a sad state of neglect. It had become a target for vandals.

Most of the windows were either broken or boarded up; the lead had been stripped from the roof and dry rot had caused several of the ceilings to collapse.

Happily, Axwell is at last (April 2008) being restored and like Paine's other villa at Belford, the hall is to be converted into twenty-three apartments with houses in the grounds. The restoration programme is a long-term project because of the building's deplorable state. However, a spokesman for the developers has said; "We hope to restore the outside of the building to its past glory, including the grand entrance".

The post-Clavering alterations to Paine's house were carried out by John Dobson, in 1817-18. During the course of his alterations John Dobson sought to make the principal entrance on the north side of the house, for he believed this was generally more sheltered from the elements. He also built a garden temple.

The south front has nine bays: the projecting three, in the centrepiece, lie under an open pediment enclosed inside which is a coat-of-arms, supported on three corbels. The south front also has a large terrace looking out towards the River Tyne.

(Featured) The main entrance on the south side.

The east front presents a different, though equally interesting, façade. Like the south front the centrepiece again has three bays under the open pediment, enclosing an identical coat-of-arms, supported on three corbels. But on either side of the centre is a single, wide (arched) bay containing a recessed, arched window.

The east front has been described as 'more villa-like'.

During the course of his alterations, in 1817-18, John Dobson sought to make the principal entrance on the north side of the house, for he believed this was generally more sheltered from the elements.

It we were able to travel back in time a few centuries, we would find that Bolam was a small town with a castle, a church and a rectory and some two hundred 'slated houses', and that it had a population of more than one thousand souls. It also, of course, had a village green. In 1305, King Edward I granted it a market and a fair.

Bolam Hall now stands on the site of the medieval castle or which now, sadly, nothing remains. But the castle, in its turn, was built within the perimeters of an ancient British camp.

Bolam Hall is not one of John Dobson's houses. It was built by Robert Horsley (who died in 1809), in 'classical style', for his daughter Charlotte Philadelphia, on her marriage to the Hon. John W Beresford. Horsley, together with his son-in-law, was instrumental in hastening the decline of the village: houses were removed to provide open views from the Hall.

The west wing: note the pedimented stone doorway with Tuscan columns and slightly recessed entrance, in the centre; the four sash windows on the ground floor and the five on the first floor all have architrave surrounds.

The Hall is a two-storeyed building of five bays, 'rather plain but in a beautiful setting'.

The East wing (featured) has a Venetian window above the entrance door, four tripartite windows on the ground floor and five sash windows on the first floor, which, like those in the west wing, have architrave surrounds.

In 1816, John Dobson was employed by the Hon. John Beresford (later Lord Decies) to lay out an artificial lake at Bolam, together with the "necessary islands and adjoining plantations". From the Northumberland County Archives we learn that 1849 Dobson became involved in a legal dispute concerning the "loss of timber profits" (as a result of alleged neglect) from the trees he had planted in 1816-18 and he was summoned as an expert witness.

In his subsequent affidavit John Dobson expressed the opinion (more than once) that proper attention had not been paid to thinning out the trees, to allow for proper growth.

Indeed, Dobson complained that his original landscape design had suffered as a consequence of this neglect – "the trees are spindled up and without lateral branches and the undergrowth destroyed, thereby exposing the lake to view from the public road".

The recurring substance of his affidavit was his allegation that the trees had suffered badly from neglect and, moreover, he was able to substantiate his claim with clear evidence, evidence which patently demonstrated his competence and experience as a talented landscape gardener; a talent no doubt inherited from his late father, John Dobson Senior, who was himself an accomplished landscape gardener.

Bolam Country Park, as it now is, attracts many kinds of wild fowl at all times of the year – mute swans, Canada geese, moorhens, grebes, coot, mallards, tufted ducks and goosanders, amongst others. Tomlinson colourfully described the lake as "a picturesque sheet of water with some pretty creeks, islands and promontories, surrounded by trees and flowering shrubs and frequented by several species of wild fowl".

"Ducks are a-dabbling,
Up tails all."

(Kenneth Grahame)

The Priory Church of St Peter and St Paul   (Brinkburn, near Rothbury)

Brinkburn was already known by that name when, in the reign of Henry I, William de Bertram of Mitford selected it for the site of a Convent of Austen Canons – about the year 1135. With the consent of his wife and sons, he commissioned Osbert Colutarius to begin building for Sir Ralph the priest and his brethren.

The Bertrams made valuable grants of land to the Priory but the 'Chartulary' (a register or record book kept in a monastery) shows they were often impoverished by Scottish raids. Legend has it that on one occasion the Scots had been unable to find the Priory, hidden among the thick woodland and so the marauders turned their horses northwards. The monks, grateful for their deliverance, rang the deep bells of the monastery their relief. Alas the sounds of the bell guided the raiders back to leave behind them fire and slaughter in the peaceful valley. The canons complained often and long (and with good reason) about their poverty – a Commissioners' report of 1552 supported their complaint. In 1556, however, the Prior was found guilty of immoral conduct and his canons guilty of "venerating a girdle of St Peter"

The convent was dissolved and the Priory passed into lay hands and a house was established on the site. The church remained in use but began to decay (in the 17th century the roof of the Priory fell in at the south-west angle) and regular services lapsed in 1683, although burials continued. Despite its troubles, Brinkburn remained a beautiful blending of the richest Norman work with purest Early English.

It is earlier than Hexham Abbey and it is possible its lancet windows have been copied in many churches in South Northumberland.

The nave has three doorways; the most architecturally exciting is that on the north side.
It has, according to one writer, "an exuberant display of late Norman ornament".
Above the beautiful arched doorway, in the gable, is a Gothic arcade of three trefoiled-
pointed arches: bands of dogtooth run down the angles of the projection.

The Priory House (top), with its huge central bow and six Georgian-Gothic windows, inserted into the original east side of the house by John Dobson, who worked here at Brinkburn (on both the Priory and the house) between 1830 and 1837.

The large central windows, with their interesting tracery, match those on either side of the bow in everything but size.

The 'manor house' had been extended, in 1810-11, by Major Hodgson-Cadogan's father, "in a plain Gothic style".

John Dobson rebuilt ('remarkably successfully', so it was said) the older part of the house in a castellated-Gothic manner, a style he was to employ at both Beaufront Castle, near Hexham, and Holme Eden Abbey Warwick Bridge, near Carlisle.

The main entrance (bottom), on the north side is through a heavy Tudor-style, arched portico: both portico and the tower behind are battlemented and have mullioned and transomed windows.

Drawings of Dobson's alterations and additions to the house can be seen in the Laing Gallery, Newcastle upon Tyne.

The house, built between 1603-20, during the reign of James I, but probably incorporating 'older parts', is essentially that built by William Blakiston.

The Hall passed to Sir William Bowes, through his marriage to Elizabeth Blakiston in 1692 and thence to Sir William's third son, George Bowes, and later still, in 1767, to the ninth Early of Strathmore.

It was enlarged on the north side (featured), probably in the mid-18th century and, again, on the east side, in 1805.

Meadows and Waterson refer to John Dobson's plans for the addition of a conservatory for the tenth Earl, writing that "in 1813 Dobson made designs for an ambitious conservatory adjoining the house in a …. Castellated manner." The Earl had commissioned Dobson to design a large conservatory which was to be added to the west end of the house. This charming building of cast-iron and glass was to be fed by rainwater and heated by hot air from an adjacent furnace: it would be possible to walk directly from the house into the conservatory full of luxuriant and exotic plants.

Meadows and Waterson claim the work was never done though "his (Dobson's) drawings of Gibside provide evidence for its appearance and plan at that date".

The north elevation overlooks the Derwent Valley.

In 1814 John Dobson proposed minor alterations (though Lyall Wilkes describes them as 'large' and quotes 1813, 1815 and 1856 when work was carried out by the Newcastle architect). The Newcastle Daily Journal also mentions work done in 1856. In its obituary on January 16th, 1865, it says that Dobson made alterations to the 17th century house for W Hutt MP some nine years or so before the architect's death. The drawings referred to by Meadows and Waterson, relating to the proposed conservatory, are to be found in the Durham County Records Office (D/St/X46a, 81); but an account also exists in the same record office for "unknown work" in 1818, for which John Dobson was paid the sum of fifty pounds (D/St/V1513,pp14,15).

The south front was rebuilt by John Bowes (the tenth Earl), who removed the third storey and replaced the front with a high battlemented parapet (work by Alexander Gilkie), pierced with huge crosses.

Nevertheless, the careful reconstruction of the main porch and the character of the five bays of square mullioned windows denotes a sympathetic respect for Jacobean architecture.

After the death of the wife of the tenth Earl (mother of John Bowes), in 1860, the house was little used.

After the death of John Bowes in 1885 the house was never again occupied by the family.

The late Queen Elizabeth, the Queen Mother, could recall occasional picnics being taken at Gibside at the beginning of the 20th century but, obviously, these would be held in the grounds not the house.

In 1889 there had been plans mooted to covert the Hall into a hydropathical establishment but nothing had come of them.

Land-army girls were billeted in the house during the 1914-18 war but by then its roof was failing and it lacked both plumbing and sanitation.

It was gutted in 1920 and a large fireplace….. supporting a large mantel, decorated with the Blakiston arms, was transferred to Glamis Castle, where it was installed in the billiards room.

Gibside had been a roofless shell since 1920 but "it still preserves the character of a long, low, Jacobean-style building capped by an exaggeratedly high castellated parapet."

The wing added in 1805 (probably by David Stephenson, Newcastle's leading architect at that time) is to the right of the entrance front.

The entrance porch, though reconstructed in 1805, probably represents the 17th century porch, with Tuscan columns on high pedestals, the Royal Arms of James I flanked by sculpted figures… the initials of William and Jane Blakiston and the date, 1620.

The Church of St Andrew   (Bywell)

The church is said to have the finest Saxon tower in the country: the nave and the chancel have been much reconstructed since they were first built in the 13th century. Little original work remains – only the "lepers squint" and the piscine in the south transept.

The church was altered by John Dobson in 1830 and again in 1850.

After the Normal Conquest of 1066 Bywell became the meeting place of the two baronies of Bolbeck and Balliol. Walter of Bolbeck founded Blanchland Abbey, in 1165, and he gave the right to appoint a vicar at St Andrew's to the "white Canons" of Blanchland. St Peter's Church (nearby) was given by the Balliols to the black-robed Benedictine monks of Durham which explains why, down through the ages, the two churches have been known locally and affectionately as the 'white church' and the 'black church'.

Both churches pre-date the Norman Conquest and there is ample evidence to support this assertion. For example, writing in 1104 Simeon of Durham says Ecgberht was consecrated Bishop of Lindisfarne here, at "Bigwell", in 803, after the Danes had sacked the Holy Island of Lindisfarne.

There is even evidence (though admittedly not much) that an earlier church was founded on this site, by Wilfred of Hexham, in the 7th century. There is evidence of the church's roughly circular graveyard. But, most compelling, there is the wonderful Saxon tower.

The tower, which appears to be built partly of re-used stones from the Roman Wall, is fifty-five feet high and consists of four stages. The lower stages are earlier than 850 and the upper stages date from the tenth and early eleventh centuries.

The principal building material of both the tower and the church walls is coarse grained sandstone varying in colour from predominant cream to yellow and brown with some reddish tone blocks.

There is no western doorway to the tower: it is entered from the nave by a 13th century archway. The main body of the church dates mostly from the 13th century, though it was extensively enlarged and repaired in 1871, having previously been altered by John Dobson in both 1830 and 1850 (Pevsner).

The architect responsible for the later restoration is believed to have been R J Johnson of Newcastle, of whom it has been written, "he did much of the creditable church work in the county in the late 19th century". Certainly, the north transept, vestry, sanctuary arcading, communion rails, pulpit and lectern, all date from this period.

One last word about the tower. In an inventory written in 1552 it was said that there were "two belles in the stepell": the smaller had been cast c.1400, the larger c.1550.

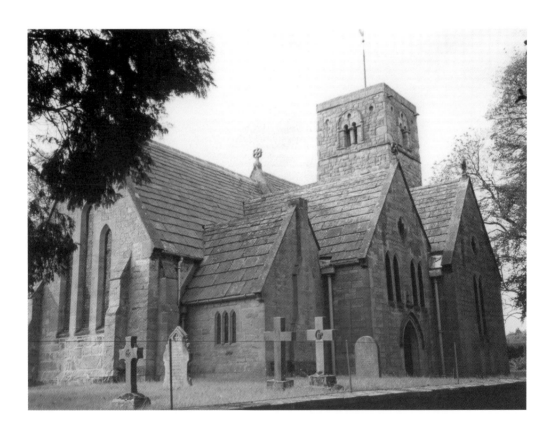

The 'white church' of St Andrew, Bywell.

At the time of the late Victorian restoration (1871) twenty-five, 12th and 13th century grave or coffin covers were incorporated into the external walls of the church or taken inside and used as lintels.

Of the twenty-five 'slabs' eighteen were re-set in the external north wall and the other seven used as lintels over windows and doorways, inside the church. Each cover bears a cross often accompanied by some other emblem, denoting the trade or the rank of the person interred

Of the covers with emblems nine have a sword (denoting the right to bear arms?) and another nine bear a pair of shears (a female emblem): the remainder show a variety of emblems –a pair of tongs, a hunting horn, a book or lady's work-box and so on

At the beginning of the 1900s ten covers were transferred from outside the church 'for their protection'; to save them from the vagaries of our oft inclement weather and the consequent erosion.

St Andrew's was declared redundant in 1973.

The only medieval coffin covers still to be seen on the external walls of the church are these two fine examples, one either side of the north door: the remainder are now (2007) all to be found inside the church.

In the 16th century a Tudor house was added to the existing medieval castle already occupying the site, by 'Ser John Fenwicke'.

The last of the Fenwicks (Cavaliers and Jacobites) to own Wallington was Sir John Fenwick, who was executed in 1697 on a charge of plotting to kill King William III.

Some years previously, however, the house had been purchased from Sir John (by now a 'landless and broken man') by Sir William Blackett who, immediately on purchase of the estate, both castle and Tudor manor house and, in 1688, began the construction of the present building – modelled on a French chateau.

The house remained the possession of the Blackett's until 1777 when, on the death of Sir Walter Blackett (who died childless but whose sister Julia had married Sir George Trevelyan, in 1733) the estate passed into the hands of the Trevelyans – a Cornish family by origin.

Sir Walter Trevelyan owned Wallington from 1846-79.   At that time the house surrounded a damp, dark and dingy courtyard

John Dobson was presumably chosen, in 1855, to convert the courtyard into useable living space because of his years of experience with the houses of the Trevelyans' neighbours…. Angerton, Mitford, Meldon, etc. Dobson's design was in a subdued, Italianate style, thoroughly appropriate to the rest of the house (described as one of the most beautiful 18th century houses in Northumberland), though "the hall impinges little on the older rooms, with their exceptionally fine 18th century plasterwork". Only the staircase had to be rebuilt to accommodate the 'hall', which rises in two tiers of arcades towards a coffered ceiling.

It was John Ruskin who had suggested the courtyard could be roofed over and the present, beautifully-lighted picture gallery (or hall) was created under Ruskin's directions.   Indeed, John Dobson's designs had to be submitted to Ruskin for his approval as he, Ruskin, was Lady Pauline Trevelyan's mentor 'in all things artistic'.

It would be interesting to know what Dobson's thoughts were regarding this arrangement but, perhaps wisely, he kept them to himself.

The pictures, painted between 1856-60, around the north and south walls of the gallery are all by William Bell Scott, a pre-Raphaelite artist who, at the time of his work at Wallington, had been Master of the Government School of Design, in Newcastle, since 1843. The eight paintings portray scenes from Northumberland's history throughout the centuries, starting with the Roman Wall.   Like Lady Waterford's paintings in Ford Village Hall Scott featured local people (some celebrated, others from ordinary walks of life) in several of his pictures.   For example, in his picture 'Building the Roman Wall', the centurion is a portrait of John Clayton, of Chesters, Newcastle's Town Clerk. Another character portrayed on the same canvas is Dr John Collingwood Bruce, the recognised authority on all things related to the Roman Wall.

Mr William Henry Charlton of Hesleyside is portrayed in 'The Spur in the Dish', a scene in a Border castle anytime during the Middle Ages. A friend of Scott's, one Miss Boyd, appears on both 'the Spur..' and 'Grace Darling', whereon she represents the Longstone heroine, helping her father William rescue the survivors of the Forfarshire, wrecked on Harcar Rock, in 1838.

Scott himself appears in a painting titled 'Bernard Gilpin' and Lady Pauline features in 'The Descent of the Danes'. But others, perhaps less instantly recognisable, were also used as models – a clergyman and a porter in 'King Egfrid and Cuthbert's: a gamekeeper and a piper in 'The Spur in the Dish', and three figures hammering in 'Iron and Coal' were men from George Stephenson's workshop on Tyneside. John Ruskin is said to have designed the balustrade on the first floor. The stone pilasters between the paintings were decorated with oats and wheat and blue cornflowers, by lady Pauline Trevelyan (nee Jermyn), 'a brilliant and sensitive woman', her friends and the ubiquitous Ruskin. The upper spandrels portray the heads of eminent men who have made an impressions, of one kind or another, on our County's long and glorious history… among whom are shown the Emperors Hadrian and Severus (who built and repaired the Wall); Alcuin (a brilliant scholar at the Court of Charlmagne); Bishop Ridley (burnt at the stake for his religious beliefs, in 1555); the Earl of Derwentwater (beheaded in 1716 for his part in the Jacobite Rebellion the previous year); Nathaniel Crewe (a notorious time-served Bishop… of Durham, of whom it was said, "he was neither a brilliant political nor ecclesiastical character and there was nothing in his life became him like the leaving of it, sine he then founded the Bamburgh Trust".); Admiral Lord Collingwood (of Trafalgar fame); John and William Scott (later Earl Eldon, Lord Chancellor of England and his brother Lord Stowell); Thomas Bewick (the celebrated engraver); Earl 'Reform Bill' Grey (whose statue stands at the top of Grey Street, which was renamed after him) and George Stephenson (the 'Father of the Railway').

The Clock Tower: Wallington Hall

61

In 1855 the courtyard was roofed in and given an Italian arcade on square pillars, and an arched gallery. The architect was John Dobson.

In medieval times there was a castle on this site at Wallington. In the middle of the 16th century the Fenwicks added a Tudor house to the castle (the cellars of the present building contains the original foundations).

Sir William Blackett, a rich Newcastle businessman, bought Wallington in 1684. He demolished the Fenwicks' Tudor house and in 1688 began to build the house which stands (its exterior almost unchanged) today. Wallington Hall is designed on the lines of a French chateau and is an exactly square building – each of the four frontages measures one hundred and twenty feet.

The west front – with its ten bays and projecting wings.

The Hall is built of honey-coloured sandstone and has a hipped roof. The south front has nine bays with a three-bay, slightly projecting, centrepiece with pediment. It too has quoins. The doorway is capped with a broken pediment.

The east front is beautifully symmetrical in its appearance: two storeys with eleven bays, the two bays at either end project slightly. It has quoins and the doorway has two Tuscan columns and a pediment.

The gargoyles on the east lawn are said to have been used as ballast in one of Blackett's coal-boats returning to the Tyne from London.

1. The Prison and Court House: Belford.

The small prison and Court House, still standing on Belford's main street, has been attributed to John Dobson. The date is believed to be 1823.

2.   St Michael's, Bishopwearmouth (now Sunderland Minster).

3.   The Clock Tower, Wallington Hall, Cambo.
     In 1815, John Dobson was commissioned to convert the courtyard into what is
     now the magnificent picture gallery.
     Wallington Hall is now a National Trust property

4. St. Michael and All Angels, Ford. The church pre-dates the nearby castle and was extensively restored by John Dobson, in 1853.

5. St Mary's Church, Gateshead. After Dobson restored the church, following the disastrous fire of 1854, he received a letter of commendation from the Bishop of Durham.

6. The Village Cross, Holy Island

In the village square (formerly the market place) stands this beautiful stone Celtic cross; twelve feet high it was rebuilt by Dobson – at H C Selby's expense – in 1828 … as the inscription reads. It stands on the pedestal of 'St Cuthbert's Cross', erected by Bishop Aethelwold

7.   St John's, Meldon.
Originally an early thirteenth century church, restored by Dobson in 1849. The triple lancet window in the east end and the bellcote are both features of this restoration.

8.   St Andrew's, Winston-on-Tees. Much of the church (except the south-west tower) was rebuilt by Dobson in 1848.

9.   The Archbold Monument   St. Nicholas' Cathedral, Newcastle upon Tyne

The monument consists of a marble bust on a base, set in a roundel surmounted by
a pediment and underneath which is an inscribed plaque. It was erected by Miss
Jane Archbold in memory of her brother James, who died on the 2nd January,
1849, aged 68 years. James Archbold, born in Newcastle, was Sheriff in 1840,
Mayor in 1846 and for several years both an Alderman and a Magistrate. The
monument is situated in an alcove against the west wall. A small shop was
installed in the Cathedral c.1978/9, in this alcove which, in effect, has made it
impossible to take either a frontal photograph of the monument or read its
inscription. Moreover, it has permanently blocked exit from and entrance to the
Cathedral by the south door.

The Newcastle Courant of July 21st, 1854, describes John Dobson's monument as
'classical': the date is believed to be 1849.

JUSTUS PROPOSITI TENAX

TO THE MEMORY OF
ROBERT HOPPER WILLIAMSON ESQUIRE
LATE CHANCELLOR OF THE COUNTY OF DURHAM
AND RECORDER OF NEWCASTLE UPON TYNE
WHO DIED ON THE 8th DAY OF JANUARY MDCCCXXXV AGED LXXX YEARS

IN HIS CHARACTER
AS A MAGISTRATE AND A JUDGE HE WAS PATIENT LABORIOUS DISCRIMINATING JUST
IN HIS INTERCOURSE WITH THE PROFESSION HE WAS KIND FRANK OBLIGING
FOLDLY TO UNLOCK THE TREASURES OF HIS WELL-STORED MIND
AND GENEROUS IN BESTOWING THEM ON ALL WHO SOUGHT HIS AID
ILS ATTACHMENT TO THE JUDICIAL INSTITUTIONS OF THE COUNTRY WAS WARM AND SINCERE
HE APPRECIATED THEIR VALUE AND KNEW THEIR IMPORTANCE TO
THE RIGHTS AND LIBERTIES OF THE PEOPLE
IN FINE DURING A LIFE PROTRACTED BEYOND THE USUAL TERM ALLOTTED TO MAN
HE SECURED AN ELEVATED SITUATION IN SOCIETY WITH
MOST DISTINGUISHED HONOUR TO HIMSELF
AND BENEFIT TO HIS COUNTRY

THIS MONUMENT WAS ERECTED BY HIS PROFESSIONAL AND PERSONAL FRIENDS
MDCCCXXXVII

10.   The Williamson Monument   St Nicholas' Cathedral, Newcastle upon Tyne

Robert Hopper Williamson, Magistrate, Judge and one-time Chancellor of the County Palatine of Durham and Recorder of Newcastle upon Tyne, died on the 13th January 1835, at the age of eighty years.

The monument, which is situated at the west wall of the Cathedral, near the south door, is mentioned in the Newcastle Courant of June 23rd, 1837, where it is simply described as 'classical'.

The monument was designed by John Dobson, in 1837, though the actual sculpture – 'a seated figure on a comfortably padded chair' – is by Dunbar.

The medieval church was greatly restored, in 1818, by John Dobson, who rebuilt the east end.

St. John's has an elaborate roof with traceried beams, big floral bosses and figures of saints. One window shows St. John of Beverley healing a dumb boy: another shows St. George slaying a dragon.

The gravestone, to the west of the church, shows the resting place of William Cuthbert who (between 1837-41), commissioned Dobson to build the fine castellated mansion that is Beaufront Castle, on the site of an earlier Elizabethan house.

Described as "the most impressive house of Dobson's early years," the Hall is built on the site of an earlier house.

Built in 1818 for Henry Taylor it is described as a plain, classical house with a five-bay front and a Greek Doric porch 'in antis'. The house was enlarged and remodelled in 1910.

"Doxford would appear to be the first of Dobson's houses that benefited from the exceptional masonry skills that (Sir Charles) Monck bequeathed to Northumberland following the completion of Belsay Hall.

Dobson had good reason to acknowledge the influence of the masons employed at Belsay."

(Faulkner and Greg)

This lovely Greek Doric porch with its two fluted columns forms the main entrance on the south elevation.

'….. the charming little external stairs, in the angle of the north and east wings'.

The Bridge on the Fell is an early 18th century construction. It lies on the B6348 road from Wooler to Belford, a quarter of a mile or so east of the village of Chatton, and crosses the River Till. The bridge has three segmental arches and triangular cutways. Originally it was some ten feet wide but in 1857 the arches were doubled in thickness by John Dobson.

The Old Vicarage (now Longstone House)   (Chatton)

The present Old Vicarage, now known as Longstone House and divided into two separate dwellings – East and West Longstone House – was built by John Dobson, in 1845, on the site of the former Vicarage House. The Reverend Matthew Burrell, Vicar of Chatton at that time had written to the Bishop of Durham (in whose Diocese the Vicarage lay), asking his permission to have the old Vicarage rebuilt.
He did not, however, receive either the Bishop's sympathetic support for his proposal or the response he had hopefully expected – far from it!

Edward, Bishop of Durham, wrote an 'Instrument' (dated the 4th of July, 1844), addressed to the Reverend Luke Yarcar (Vicar of Chillingham) and the Reverend Henry Parker (Rector at Ilderton) and in it he expressed grave concerns about the situation at 'the Vicarage House' at Chatton.

He commissioned these two worthy clerics to "make enquiry into the state and condition of the Buildings upon the Glebe, belonging to the said Benefice, at the time the said Matthew Burrell entered upon the same". The general tone of his 'Instrument' clearly illustrates the Bishop's deep misgivings and seems to suggest that perhaps all was not well at Chatton. The brief of the two appointed clergymen was quite explicit. The Bishop wanted to know "as soon as conveniently may be", whether "the said Matthew Burrell hath by wilful negligence suffered such buildings to go out of repair", and he further instructs that they must appraise him of "the amount of damage which such buildings have sustained by the wilful neglect of the said Matthew Burrell". Strong language indeed! Their eventual reply to the Bishop demonstrates that the two clergymen (Yarcar and Parker) had not only conducted a full enquiry but that they had reached the same conclusion expressed, some four months later, by the architect John Dobson.

In Burrell's defence, however, they pointed out in their reply to the Bishop that he had only "entered the said Living (ie Chatton)… about the month of July, 1844" (so that, on the surface at least, it did seem rather unfair to blame the man for the state of the building which had suffered cruel neglect for many years previous to his occupancy). The reverend gentlemen also found that "the state of the building is extremely old and rudely built… and of an inferior quality, the decay of which had been increased by the want of ventilation and proper drainage…." We also learn from their reply that Matthew Burrell was apparently to receive a sum of almost one hundred and five pounds 'compensation' from the previous incumbent at Chatton 'for dilapidations' (a sum, we suppose was designed to help meet the costs of essential repairs to the building), but that this money had not been used for the purpose for which it was intended.

There are also "law charges" mentioned in connection with the 'settlement' offered by the previous occupant but these are neither elaborated nor clarified.

Whatever mystery may or may not be attached to these disclosures, a mystery it must unfortunately remain, for there are no further papers available to 'lighten our darkness', as it were, and bring the story to a satisfactory conclusion. Sadly, we must remain in ignorance.

In any event, all of this information was duly relayed to the Bishop by Reverend Yarcar and Reverend Parker, in their reply of September 24th (1844), after an enquiry which had taken some three weeks to complete.

In a sworn affidavit, the following January (1845) John Dobson affirmed that he had examined the Vicarage House at Chatton "and finds that the whole is in such a state of dilapidation that it cannot be put into a habitable state of repair".

Mr Dobson then went on to justify his (professional) opinion with telling facts: "The masonry… is so bad that what can be got will scarce repay the cost of pulling down the building and remove the rubbish… The main timbers, flooring and other woodwork are in such a state of decay that no part can be used in the construction of a new building…"

In a second affidavit (of January 16th, 1845), to the Reverend Luke Yarcar (who, as well as being the Vicar of Chillingham, was also a Justice of the Peace), John Dobson declared that such, indeed, was the state of the Old Vicarage House that old timber and other materials (doors, windows, boilers etc) that might be salvaged and were 'fit to be employed' in his proposed new building, had a value of only £42-2-0.

Work began in 1845 and the estimate of expenses for the proposed new Vicarage (the present Longstone House) amounted, after deductions for useable old materials, to £2,453-16-3.

John Dobson's architect's fee was £70!

There were two pele-towers here, in 1416 and 1542.

One was occupied by the Parish Clergyman and is incorporated in the present Vicarage.

The gable at the west end of the house has four steps while, interestingly, the east gable has five.

Lambton Castle   (Chester-le-Street)

Many of the Lambton Castle's problems in the middle of the 19th century stemmed from the fact that the castle was built over forgotten mine-workings. The castle had been enlarged by Ignatius Bonomi in the 1820s but, by 1854 the building showed distinct signs of imminent collapse. In short, it was "almost wrecked by subsidence".
It is perhaps the ultimate compliment to John Dobson's talents as an engineer, that, at the age of sixty-nine, he should have been called in, in 1857, to underpin the castle and to design major new extensions to it.
He also designed new reception rooms around the Great Hall.

71

"A picturesque house, which is the product of several rebuildings, the first between 1798 and 1801 by Joseph Bonomi, and later by John Dobson – begun in 1857 and completed by his son-in-law, Sydney Smirke, between 1862-66."
In the 1930s the house was reduced in size.

When, by the mid-1850s, the castle was in imminent danger of collapse, Ignatius Bonomi was made the scapegoat. His 'bad' designs were blamed for the castle's problems when, in fact, it was because it had been built on disused mine-workings, which are the real cause of the problem. The task of 'shoring up' the building was given to John Dobson and his son-in-law, Sydney Smirke, and a small fortune was spent filling up the old seams and stabilising the foundations.

The entrance on the north side, showing the porte-cochère and the west front.

The west front of the castle.

Lambton Castle came into existence... towards the end of the 18th century, and was the result of the castellation of a Hall built only forty years previously and, as Nikolaus Pevsner has remarked, has nothing genuine about it (not even its name!) save its beautiful, biscuit-coloured stone: but it remains, nevertheless, a mock-medieval triumph.

Lambton Castle: the magnificent port-cochère

Chollerton Grange   (Chollerton)

John Dobson worked at Chollerton Grange (the Vicarage, as it was then), in both 1830
and 1847, for two vicars – father and son.
Dr Frank Atkinson is of the opinion that the Vicarage "is of two builds, largely by John
Dobson". Lyall Wilkes also assumed that only part of the house was Dobson's work.
The present owner insists, however (and he should know), that the work is entirely that
of John Dobson.
Drawings, coded 1875/c, are to be found in the Northumberland County Records Office
at Woodhorn Colliery Museum.

Chollerton Grange: a two-storeyed, hipped-roof building with an open, projecting pediment. It has three bays, though the ground floor window on the left, unlike the others is tripartite.

Fallodon Hall   (Christon Bank)

In the first half of the 17th century a Puritan merchant from Berwick, named Sakeld, built a small country house at Fallodon.

In 1704 Thomas Wood bought the estate and around 1730 he pulled down Sakeld's house and built a red-brick mansion, with stone facings – the bow on the south side is a later addition (c.1796?)

After Wood's death, in 1755, the house passed to the Grey family and it was during the occupancy of Sir Edward Grey (later Viscount Grey of Fallodon) that the house was practically destroyed by fire, in May 1917. Trevelyan tells us that after the fire "only the furniture, pictures and books on the ground floor were saved." After living in the kitchen wing until the (1914-18) war was over Grey painstakingly restored his beloved home, using the old bricks, in the same general style as before but with only two storeys instead of the previous three and with some changes in the ground plan of the rooms.

The south elevation (left): the 'bow' was added at the end of the 18th century.
John Dobson's east wing (right).

John Dobson's east wing of 1815 is of dressed sandstone.   The present owner is at a loss to understand why the architect did not build it of red brick, in keeping with the rest of the house.

Craster Tower   (Craster)

The south front.

The Craster family has lived on this site since at least the 12th century. Edmund Craster was the owner in 1415 but Albert, the founder of the Craster 'dynasty' was in possession of Craster before 1168.

As members of the same family are living here today (2008) this means that Albert's descendents have occupied the Tower for more than eight centuries. In 1837 Thomas Wood-Craster inherited the property and adopted the name. It was probably he who enlarged the garden and created the ha-ha ditch. He added a third floor to the east wing and also altered all the chimneys in the south wing (having had persistent problems with rising damp, a problem that apparently still exists today). He also made the open screen partition in the library and built the bay-window on the east side for which, in 1839, he employed John Dobson – see drawings in the NCRO; ZCR Maps 55.

The south front (over page), with quoins at both ends, is faced with square whinstone and it has a central, open pediment. The windows have heavy architraves and the central window, above the doorway, is pedimented. Many of the house's characteristics suggest the hand of Newcastle architect William Newton – the floating cornice above the central, second-floor window, for example is also a feature of Shawdon Hall (near Glanton), which many believe is also the work of Newton. The central doorway is tripartite, with Tuscan pilasters, and it too, is surmounted by an open pediment.

The beautiful south front with it open pediment (left) and the much plainer east side with the bay-window added by John Dobson, in 1839.

The three-storeyed, battlemented Tower (the battlements, incidentally, are a fairly modern addition), certainly existed as far back as the beginning of the 15th century – it is mentioned in the county's list of castles, fortalices and towers, compiled in 1415.

It has a ten feet high, vaulted basement and a wheel-stair in the south-east corner where a wall is almost six and a half feet thick.

The adjacent east wing has four feet thick walls which, Pevsner believes, suggest a medieval or 16th century date, but this part of the Tower was extended and remodelled in the nineteenth century.

The Tower has two rows of three lancet windows on the west face, the central, larger window has intersecting tracery.

In 1769 the two-and-a-half-storeyed, five-bay 'new house' was added to the south side of the Tower.

Arcot Hall   (Dudley, near Cramlington)

The Newcastle daily Journal of January 16th, 1865, claims that 'in the 1820s John Dobson made additions to the 18th century house at Arcot, which is now and has been for a number of years, a Golf Club. It is an 'L-plan' house. Its centre bow (on the west front) is capped by a lead dome, similar to that on William Stokoe's Hartford Hall, near Bedlington.

This part of the house (the bow) was added by John Dobson for George Shum-Storey, an Indian adventurer who was present at the siege of Arcot, near Madras: it seems likely, therefore, that this inspired him to choose the name he did for his residence.

The three-bay, three-storeyed south front has a most attractive Roman Doric porch, said to have been added in 1805.

John Dobson's work was often impaired by a shortage of money. He complained that he had been unable to make the exterior of St Paul's (one of his largest churches) as attractive as he would have liked through lack of funds.

The church has nave, aisles and clerestory but no proper chancel. Inside, though spacious, is really very plain. The style is Gothic and the church was built in 1857, consecrated a year later.

St Paul's is now the only Christian denominational place of worship in the parish. For many years the Church Hall has been a Community Centre.

The most substantial part of the present house dates from 1828 and was designed by John Dobson… for George Dixwell Grimes, Vicar form 1822-30. Dobson refaced the south-western end of the tower, inserting new windows, and built a large extension with handsome reception rooms overlooking the garden. Best known as a classicist, in this instance Dobson chose to work in a restrained neo-Tudor style, so advanced for its time that the former vicarage is often taken to be Victorian rather than Georgian. For his new additions Dobson used the local whinstone – hard to work but very durable. Dobson built with a keen understanding of the unsparing northern climate, providing extra insulation of lath and plaster under the main floor and skilfully planning his entrance lobby to intervene between the main entrance hall and the draughts and winds from the front door.

In the late 1970s a new vicarage was built, Dobson's house by then proving inconveniently large in the changed social conditions of the 20th century and for the first time, after several centuries, the house passed out of ecclesiastical occupation.

What, then, specifically, were the alterations and additions carried out by John Dobson? H L Honeyman tells us that late in the Georgian period the brick-built, south-west wing and kitchen were added and the whole building was plastered, or 'harled', externally. Honeyman believes this, together with the present tower roof, to have been the work of James Boulter (1811-22) who after his death, was judged so severely by Archdeacon Singleton, in his visitation of 1828, who said that "Mr Boulter put a new roof on the house but never paid for it. The more recent additions have been in pitiful taste and the rooms are so low as to be hardly wholesome".

In the time of George Dixwell Grimes (1822-30) some parts of the later additions were taken down, the south-west end of the tower was refaced and a large new wing erected facing the garden, which was also altered and extended. Larger windows were inserted in the stark walls and an annexe was added to the south-west. Then the old tower was re-roofed and its interior modernised.

Finally, in the reign of George IV (1820-30), the vicarage became too mean for its vicar; part of the earlier work was removed, part re-faced and a vast new wing, containing nine rooms, a main staircase and a conservatory was constructed.

All of this information is corroborated by the present owner of the house, Mr K J Seymour-Walker, who also told me the following interesting story: Apparently, in 1832, the clerical incumbent at the time, pleading hardship applied for 'Queen Anne's Bounty' and was promised a loan of some £700, to carry out alterations. John Dobson said that if he (Dobson) pulled down the existing frontage and used the same stone to carry out this work, he could certainly complete the job for the same sum. To this proposal the Vicar was happy to agree.

The conservatory referred to by both Honeyman and Pevsner is believed by Mr Seymour-Walker to be a Dobson creation.

The roof consists of arched, cast-iron ribs (which was Dobson's style) and for this reason (the owner suggests) it could not have been built later than 1845.

Mr Dobson, as we know, was notoriously bad at keeping records of his work and, unfortunately, there appears to be no actual record of who built the conservatory, but 'the laws of probability' seem to suggest John Dobson.

The (Pele) Tower was built in 1395 at a cost of forty pounds. There are two vaults in the basement resting on a partition in the centre. The north chamber (sixteen feet seven inches N-S, by twelve feet four inches) has a fireplace, also the remains of the straight mural staircase, which has now been blocked up.

The south chamber is thirteen feet eight inches (N-S) by ten feet six inches.

The Tower is attached to the modern (sic) house and the entrance may have been on the first floor as in the north wall is a blocked opening. The battlements are there and only three feet eight inches above the water-tabling, so they would not be much use in defence.

Embleton Tower (formerly the Vicarage); extensively remodelled by John Dobson in 1828: the conservatory is on the right of the picture.

The Church of the Holy Trinity   (Embleton)

Extensive repairs and alterations were carried out on the church between 1803-05; these included a new roof and ceiling for the nave, re-flooring with flags, repairing the pews and building the churchyard wall. The 13th century chancel may well, about that time, have been replaced with a simple Georgian structure with a low, flat, whitewashed ceiling. Another addition at this time was the Grey gallery, at the west end of the north aisle.

One must assume that this work had not been of the highest standard for "there was considerable unease" and, in 1849, a meeting was convened "to consider the condition of the church and the necessity of re-seating it and the repairing of the roof and the floor thereof."

In 1849-50, John Dobson – who some twenty years previously had carried out extensive alterations to the Vicarage – was employed on a major restoration of the church.

86

Oswin Craster, in his History of Embleton church, catalogued these 'repairs' as having been an extension to the nave aisles westward as far as the west wall of the tower, so that the latter was incorporated in the body of the church: the extension of the north aisle, which then became the Grey porch or family pew, and the demolition of the Vincent Edwards and Grey galleries. All the windows were replaced by ones with 19th century decorated tracery. The nave roof was renewed but the aisle roofs were left as they were (apart from some strengthening of the southern one). The Craster porch was taken down and rebuilt on the same foundations, but higher than before. Dobson also inserted a ceiling in the lower portion of the tower, supported by stone arches.

The Church of the Holy Trinity, Embleton: John Dobson carried out a programme of repair and restoration in 1849-50.

Newton Villa Farm   (Felton, near Morpeth)

According to the present owners the house was remodelled in the mid-20th century. Previously the front door was at the top of a flight of stone steps giving access to the first floor level.

A plain, three-bay villa with recessed windows, of around 1820. Built of ashlar; the west front (featured) has a pedimented recessed doorway. The architect is believed to have been John Dobson.

The view to the east and the coast.

In 1781 Robert de Lisle of Weldon bought the estate of West Acton and part of old Felton, for the sum of £9,420.

The design of the house is attributed to the Newcastle architect, William Newton, and is very similar to Shawdon Hall, near Glanton, which has also been attributed to Newton.

The main part of the house is built of rich, cream stone. Two-storeyed, it has a seven-bay ashlar front with a three-bay centrepiece, with giant, Ionic pilasters, a fluted frieze and pediment. A flight of stone steps leads up to the central doorway, which is of the Venetian type (favoured by Robert Adam) and is a feature of both Shawdon and Backworth Hall – another Newton house.

The Newcastle Daily Journal of January 16th, 1865 tells us that in 1823 John Dobson made alterations to Acton House for Major Robert de Lisle.

The Church of St Michael and All Angels   (Ford)

This lovely thirteen-century church was standing here, overlooking the Cheviot Hills, before the castle was even built. It has, we are told, one feature which is 'archaeologically as interesting as it is architecturally successful – its bellcote.'

John Dobson carried out extensive restoration work on St Michael's in 1853-54.

Dobson was commissioned to 'modernise' the church and restore it to its basic thirteenth-century character. This he did to a remarkable degree and extremely successfully. He added the north aisle, heightened the roof of the nave, by some eight feet, and added the south entrance porch.

The windows throughout the church were redesigned and an old lancet in the west wall, which had been blocked up, was restored. It is now fitted with a stained glass window of St Michael.

The outside of the building is as fascinating as the interior. All the windows which were remodelled by Dobson in 1854 have simple hood moulds, each of which bears two stone carved faces. The Church Notes remark that "It is difficult to say whether these were the work of 19th century stonemasons, or whether they were old stone from some other building, re-used in this charming way…."

Niklaus Pevsner accuses Dobson of 'over restoring' the church. P Anderson Graham complains that 'restoration and improvement have obliterated many of (the church's) most interesting features'. On the other hand, W W Tomlinson believes that 'the work was executed with such good taste that the antique charm of the building has not been destroyed'.

The thirteenth-century church was much restored in the Victorian era. Its massive bell-turret, possibly belonging to the original building, is a rare type – built against the west wall like a big buttress and with a pyramidal cap and window-like openings for the bells.

The south entrance porch was added by John Dobson in 1854-54.

(left): A window with hood-moulding showing two of the intriguing, stone faces.

(right): Dobson enlarged the chancel arch and re-designed the chancel itself.

A neo-Norman church, by John Dobson (1845-48).

It is said St Cuthbert's was inspired by the 12th century church at Barfreston, in Kent, which Dobson had examined in 1844.

The church has a five-bay nave and a 'transitional tower' with a 'broach spire' like that on Dobson's (St Cuthbert's) church at Benfieldside, Shotley Bridge. The west wall has triple windows under a single arch. The carved 'chancel' arch is like that in St Andrew's Church, Newcastle which Dobson had restored in 1844.

There have been additions to the church since it was built by John Dobson and it is now some years since it was used as a place of worship (1999): the future of St Cuthbert's is uncertain.

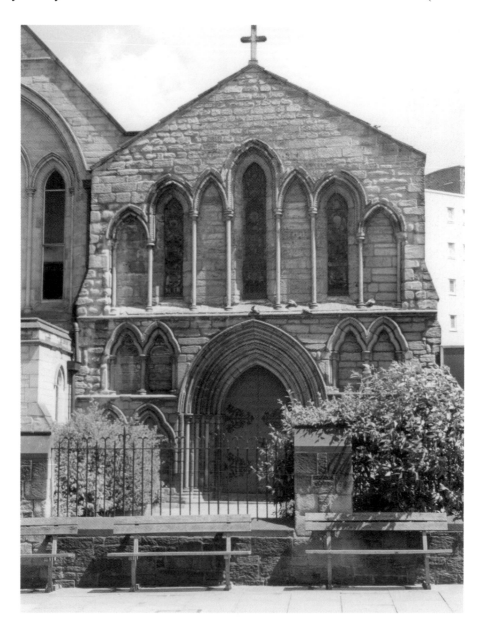

Now Trinity Community Centre, St Edmund's Chapel was restored for worship in 1837, by John Dobson.

It has a fascinating 13th century, west frontage.

The impressive doorway has two tiers of (two) 'blanked' arches. Above these and right across the face of the building is a group of seven beautiful, lancet 'stepped' arches – three with windows and four without.

The church was very badly damaged after the Great Fire of Newcastle, in October 1854. The chancel, except the east window, and the windows in the nave and aisles were all rebuilt and renewed by John Dobson, in 1855.

In 1979 the church was again gutted by fire but was again restored.

At the time of writing (2007) St Mary's had become a Visitor Centre, belonging to Gateshead Council.

Before and after restoration, following the fire of 1979 which gutted the church.

The building of Sheriff Hill Hall is inextricably linked with its owner, Matthew Plummer, and the enclosure of Gateshead Fell, in 1822.

I have already dealt fully with the career of Plummer and the repercussions of the enclosures, In the earlier edition of "Dobson", and so I feel it unnecessary and space consuming to do so again. Suffice to say that Matthew Plummer was a successful businessman who was one of the most substantial beneficiaries of the 1822 enactment. In his early days he studied agriculture and therefore pursued his farming interests until, in 1785, and due in no small part to the interest of one John Graham Clarke of Newcastle, Plummer began his successful association with that town. He started in business on the Quayside, where he did well, becoming one half of the partnership of Plummer & Greenwell, ship and insurance brokers. At that time he was living at number 96, Pilgrim Street, in Newcastle. In due course he became a partner in the Northumberland Flax Mills and mines. He invested in both land and property and was for thirty-three years Vice-Consul for the United States of America. He is probably best remembered as Chairman of the Newcastle and Carlisle Railway. His sizeable stake in the virgin Parish of Gateshead Fell gave Plummer the opportunity (as it had many other successful businessmen) to aspire to the lifestyle of a country gentleman – with the obligatory country house. He decided (or was it, perhaps, his architect's decision?) to build his house on a site on Church Road, and his architect is believed to have been John Dobson. The location and orientation of the house are clearly indicative of John Dobson. Matthew Plummer owned plenty of land in the area yet the house came to occupy a most exposed position. As Mackenzie described it, in 1834: "From its lofty situation it commands one of the finest and most extensive views in the north of England.. It embraces the whole line of the Tyne, the beautiful Vale of Ravensworth, the City of Durham and the German Ocean, both to the north and the east". Photographs of Mitford Hall (in Northumberland) and Sheriff Hill Hall (Gateshead) show a striking, indeed remarkable, resemblance in both style and appearance. Both houses were executed in a severe Greek, classical style and consisted of the typical "square block", with one wing – though Mitford is both larger and more elaborate. Sheriff Hill Hall is ashlar, with a hipped, slate roof. It is two-storeyed with three bays. The doorpiece has two Greek Ionic columns. There is some dispute on the subject of when the Hall was actually built. One claim states that Sheriff Hill Hall was designed in 1823 (the same year as Mitford Hall), and that 'the main building was completed in 1824'. The Gateshead Post (of March 20th, 1964) supports this date and in an article referring to the Hall writes…. "Although it has been standing 140 years, it is in a fine state of preservation and looks much the same as it did when Queen Victoria was but five years old".

The Queen, it should be noted, was born in 1819!

The Hall was described by Mackenzie as 'an excellent and commodious mansion'.

Matthew Plummer died on Christmas Day 1856. A little more than a year later, on February 13th, 1857, the house was advertised for sale in the Gateshead Observer. Here, details of the property are given which clearly demonstrate that the Hall was a substantial dwelling; with eleven bed and dressing rooms as well as the usual ground-floor accommodation – dining and drawing rooms, library and study; extensive servants' kitchens and office, stabling, coach-house, etc; and all standing on some three acres of land.

The 'outbuildings' which now form 34-36 Church Road, were probably added some years after the completion of the main building; the earliest record of what now forms these two houses is shown on an 1844 map of the area.

In the late 1940s the main block of the Hall became Gateshead High School which it remained until 1963 when the house and grounds were acquired by a private building firm whose intention was to convert the Hall into flats. However, in 1964, Gateshead Borough Council 'bought out' the developer at a cost of some £6000. Thereafter the Council remained undecided on the property's future, until finally, at a meeting on the 15th July, 1967, they instructed the Borough Architect to demolish the Hall.

"Thornleigh", 32 Church Road, Low Fell (the wing of the old house), is all that now remains of the original Sheriff Hill Hall.

The stone pillars marking the entrance driveway still stand on Church Road but the Hall itself was finally demolished in 1967.

Shawdon Hall is said to be one of the finest classical houses in Northumberland.

Built in 1779 for William Hargrave, on the site of the old pele tower; the tower is mentioned in 1403 and must have been a place of some importance as it was called 'castrum' in 1415, and was in 'measurable good reparacions' in 1541. There is little doubt that the 'castrum' stood in the grounds of the present hall.

The two-storeyed, seven-bay south front has a three-bay centre with steps leading up to a lovely Venetian doorway. The decorated central pediment is supported by four giant pilasters and contains an 1817 wood-carving of the Pawson coat-of-arms.

The Pawsons were wealthy landowners but rather too fond of gambling on both horses and greyhounds – hare coursing.

The story has it that if one of their horses lost a race which it was confidently expected to win, the unfortunate animal was returned to the stable-yard, shot, and its carcass disposed of in a bog on the estate. Apparently, the same fate befell a dog whose performance failed to match its master's expectations.

Eventually, though perhaps not surprisingly, the Pawsons went bankrupt and the estate had to be sold.

The architect of Shawdon Hall is unknown but on stylistic grounds the balance of probability is that it is likely to have been 'William Newton of Newcastle.

Additions and alterations to the Hall were carried out by John Dobson in 1825. Dobson made further alterations for John Pawson in 1858 and it is probable that he built the north and south lodges at this same time.

The west front has five bays with a central open pediment and a floating cornice over the first floor window beneath: there is another pediment over a wing set back to the left.

The South Lodge is linked to an arcaded screen wall.

East front.

South front.

The original house dates from the late 18th century (c.1780). The east front, of five-bays, has a central porch which is believed to be late 19th century addition.

The two-storeyed, five-bay, ashlar south front has a pedimented doorway, very like that at Glanton House.

The plainer west side of the house was extended by John Dobson, in 1829, for Henry Collingwood.

Gosforth Park   (Gosforth, Newcastle upon Tyne)

Two large gate piers, marking the west entrance to Gosforth Park, and showing the arms of the Brandling family, were designed by John Dobson for Ralph Brandling. The date is uncertain: that given by the Newcastle daily Journal of January 16th, 1865, is 1818; while Pevsner and Faulkner and Greg quote 1830.

The west entrance to Gosforth Park.

The Church of St Cuthbert   (Greenhead)

This delightful little church was designed by John Dobson and built between 1826-28. Small and rectangular with a slender octagonal spire, it was built of local stone, in the Early English style.

It was partly paid for by Nathaniel Hollingsworth, sometime poet, Vicar of Haltwhistle and one time owner of Ridley Hall.

The design, it is said, has the simplicity of genuine medieval work. In 1900 the chancel was added, the nave was restored and the spire was added to the tower.

The east window represents Christ in Majesty, King Oswald and his Queen, and some well known Northumbrian Saints of the sixth and seventh centuries.

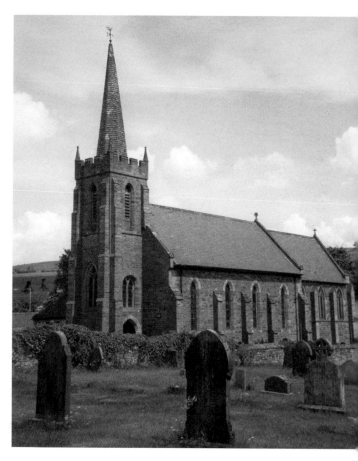

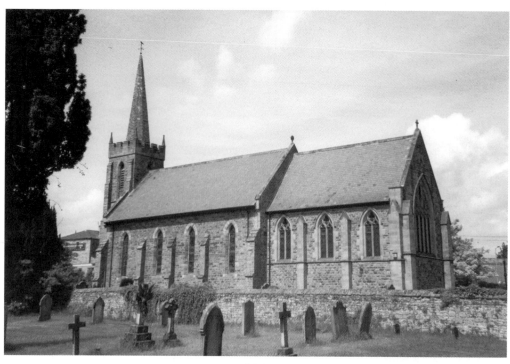

The castle stands on the summit a large oval 'motte'. It consists of a 15th century 'pele tower' and an adjoining early 19th century castellated house.

Bellister was described as a 'bastle house', which suggests it was more a pele tower than a castle. The old pele tower is now a roofless ruin. By 1715 it had become a 'ruinous building' and a century later it was described as a 'rude and crumbling mass of ruins'.

The modern house, adjacent to the old pele, was added by John Kirsopp and remodelled by John Dobson in 1827.

The house was altered again around 1890, and yet again, in 1900, after a devastating fire. In 1975 it was given to the National Trust. The present occupants have lived here since 1987.

John Dobson's work of 1827 is believed to have been the installation of the two large, upper windows on the south side of the house.

Above, we have a close-up of one of 'Mr Dobson's windows'.

The 'core' of the building, it is suggested, goes back to at least the 17th century.

In 1826, the Rector of Haltwhistle, the Reverend N J Hollingsworth commissioned John Dobson to 'make improvements' to the vicarage. The two-storeyed, canted bay-windows at either side of the south front, are most probably Dobson's alterations.

This clerical gentleman was a character of some interest. He was an amateur poet who generously provided funds for the building of the delightful Church of St Cuthbert, in the village of Greenhead. In 1826 he purchased Ridley Hall, from Thomas Bates, for the sum of £16,300.

There will always be controversy, writes Nancy Ridley, about the actual place of Bishop Nicholas Ridley's birth: two Ridley strongholds claim the honour – Willimoteswick and Unthank. Both are situated on the south side of the river and they are only a few miles apart.

At the beginning of the 16h century Ridley brothers inhabited both houses but we learn from one William Turner, a contemporary of Nicholas Ridley at Cambridge, that the future bishop always referred to his birthplace as "Willimoteswick: this declaration coming, as it were, "straight from the horse's mouth", brooks no argument.

The house, near Haltwhistle, was remodelled in 1815, 'in a plain, classical style': the architect was John Dobson.

Pevsner claims that Unthank was altered again, in 1865, 'in a free, neo-Tudor style', by the same architect: this cannot be. The date of the second alteration must have been before 1865 since Dobson died on the 8th of January that year.   Besides, Dobson's effective working life ended in 1862 after he suffered a severe stroke, so any alterations made by him could not have happened after 1861.

The Hall was altered again, in 1900 and once more in 1965 – when it was reduced in size. Nancy Ridley concludes that the extensive demolition work of 1965 left Unthank Hall "looking lonely and forlorn".

The north front.

Of the ancient pele that once stood here almost nothing has survived. John Dobson's work at Unthank is likely to be seen right of centre of the photograph, featuring mullioned, tripartite windows; the west end is of a much later date.

Harbottle Castle (House)   (Northumberland)

Stone from the nearby
medieval castle was used
to build this 17th century
fine but 'rather plain two-
storeyed five-bay villa, in
sandstone ashlar' for the
Widdrington family It was
to the east wing of the
house that John Dobson
made substantial
alterations for Thomas
Clennel in 1829.

The main entrance to the
house is on the east side
where there is a stone
porch believed by the
owners to be a Victorian
addition The original
doorway, flanked by two
Tuscan columns (part of
Dobson's design), is now
inside the porch which,
when the weather is fine is
now used as a breakfast
room.

By the time Dobson 'rebuilt' Angerton Hall, in 1842, architectural styles had changed somewhat dramatically.

Only five years previously (1837) we see the striking Gothic style of Holme Eden Abbey (in Warwick Bridge), for Peter Dixon, and Beaufront Castle (near Hexham), for William Cuthbert, displaying a profusion of towers and turrets and battlements.

The comparative, almost elegant, simplicity of Angerton is in stark contrast to what some critics considered the almost vulgar ostentation of the other two.

" – a remarkably unfussy Tudor style, with plain gables, unemphatic battlements and tall windows…"

The north side of the house.

The coat-of-arms above the large gabled porch on the north face of the Hall is that of Colonel Atkinson (described as 'a local coal-baron'), who built Angerton Hall in 1822. The house that John Dobson altered the following year (1823) he practically rebuilt in 1842 – note the date stone.

113

According to Faulkner and Greg (John Dobson, Newcastle Architect, 1787-1865), John Dobson removed galleries from The Church of the Holy Trinity (Embleton), The Priory Church of St Andrew (Hexham) and the Church of St Michael and All Angels (Houghton-le-Spring), but actually added them at The Church of St Andrew, Hartburn... in 1835. The Newcastle Daily Journal of January 16th, 1865, also makes this claim, that Dobson did indeed add galleries to the church in Hartburn, for in that year (1835) the vestrymen agreed to build a gallery to receive an organ, promised by General Sir Thomas Bradford, arranging that John Dobson should draw up the plans. He subsequently made the gallery rest on the two west pillars.

Pevsner described St Andrew's as "an interesting church, with a pre-Conquest core, late 12th to early 13th century west tower and a chancel of the same date, extended in the later 13th century".Skeletons found in the tower (forensically dated pre-1100) suggest the church was built by the Priors of Tynemouth.

Two daggers above a Maltese Cross, on the doorpost, tell of a Knight Templar Preceptory here, in 1250, and the Early English architecture speaks of little subsequent change.

Of special interest are the masons' marks – carved heads, fish, Napoleonic banners and Florentine lamps.

The west front.

It has been said of Meldon that, in plan, situation and design it is the most characteristic Dobson classical house.

Built in 1832 for Isaac Cookson III, the house is said to have cost £7,188-1-11 ... excluding the stables.

The entrance front, on the west side, is refined: it has a four-column Ionic porch and the windows have moulded surrounds.

Meldon has been described as "the last flowering of the Georgian country house tradition".

The south front, overlooking the River Wansbeck, has a canted bay in the centre.

The east front has three closely spaced windows in the centre and tripartite windows at either end.

The oldest part of the Vicarage is the 13th (?) century pele tower. The Vicarage is built of heavy, rubble masonry with a chamfered pediment, a vaulted roof and thick walls.

The south-east wing was added in 1540, to provide extra accommodation and then, in the middle of that century (1554-69) an upstairs room and a fine freestone chimney, was added.

The 'spacious and elegant' rooms, on the south side of the house, were added c.1760, by Dr Sharpe – archdeacon of Northumberland and Vicar of Hartburn from 1749-92: he also built the nearby school-house, in 1756, and the 'grotto' down by the river.

From 1834 until his death in 1845 the great Northumbrian historian, John Hodgson, lived at Hartburn Vicarage. His diary, when he moved from Kirkwhelpington to Hartburn, records that John Dobson visited the house around 1834 and produced plans to remodel the hall of the house. He also did work on the staircase (to the right of the hall as you enter through the main east door), cleverly 'arching over' the staircase: he also redesigned the coving.

Hodgson converted one of the upper rooms of the tower into a study. The Vicarage was extensively repaired in 1960.

A castellated and cement rendered building, in a highly romantic situation, near the mouth of the Dene, it had three and four-light, mullioned and hood-moulded windows and was built in 1821, by Major Anderson, from designs by John Dobson.

Originally known as Hawthorn Hive Cottage, it was remodelled as Hawthorn Tower by Thomas Moore of Sunderland, c.1850.

The house was occupied until the 1939-45 War, but soon afterwards it was abandoned and, in time, it became ruinous.

In the early 1970s two young lads, aged about fourteen or fifteen, were climbing on the tower when one fell and tragically was killed. Easington Council then took the decision to demolish the building.

The aerial photograph (reproduced by kind permission of Easington District Council), over-page, was taken some time in the 1950s: unfortunately, there is no record of the exact date.

Hawthorn Tower

Not all of John Dobson's work met with universal acclaim and approval. Reconstruction work on St Nicholas' Cathedral (as it now is) lead to his being taken to task by his fellows in the Newcastle Society of Antiquaries. Rebuilding work done at St Gregory's, Kirknewton was vehemently opposed by his hitherto friend and supporter, the distinguished architect, Anthony Salvin. His restoration work on the Church of St Michael and All Angels, Ford, has been criticised for "having obliterated many of the most interesting features" and for "over-restoring the church".

But perhaps his most controversial piece of restoration work, arousing much vociferous opposition, was carried out on Hexham Abbey.

There has been a church on this site for more than thirteen centuries. Queen Etheldreda of Northumbria granted land to Wilfrid, Bishop of York, c.674, and he built a Benedictine Abbey. This was replaced in Norman times by an Augustine Priory, c.1170-1250, and much of the church we see today dates from that time.

John Dobson had been engaged in work of one kind or another, on St Andrew's since 1817 and in 1828 he restored the Abbey's east window, overlooking the Market Place. In 1858, however, he finally removed the unusual late Gothic, five-light structure, with a 'rose' as its centrepiece and replaced it with two tiers of triple lancets, a design based on that at Whitby Abbey.

Pevsner, rather mutely, described the result as "disappointing". Faulkner and Greg describe the effect as "hard, neat and academically correct", adding that, although it was approved by many of his local colleagues "it was censured by some of the journals of the time in the severest terms".

W W Tomlinson is even more incensed and writes that "the Abbey has suffered much from destructive restoration". He adds that "Vandals have impaired its Gothic beauty. The east end was restored in a barbarous manner ..."

The Newcastle Daily Chronicle, of January 9th, 1865, gives a somewhat different version of the 'facts', however: In 1817, Dobson was called in by Colonel Beaumont to restore the east end of Hexham Abbey Church, Dobson urged that the east end, a fine example of the Early Pointed style, should be restored in harmony with the rest of the building, but his design was overruled and the Catherine Wheel window of a late and debased style was consequently replaced. Dobson, thirty years later, demolished his own work and restored the harmony of the building by introducing the tiers of lancet windows similar to the Abbey Church in Whitby, which Dobson considered of the same approximate date.

Beaufront Tower occurs in the list of castles and fortalices of both 1415 and 1541, though by 1547 it was styled a manor.

In 1547 it was the seat of David Carnaby Esq. Afterwards, it became the residence of the Errington family, who built a rather splendid mansion on the site.

At the end of the 18th century John Errington spent some £20,000 on his gardens, lawns, etc – a veritable fortune at that time. Yet, when he died, the new owner – William Cuthbert – demolished the house and commissioned John Dobson to build a new house on the site, "in the domestic castellated style" … which he did, between 1836-41.

Part of the old 16th century house was incorporated into Dobson's 19th century building. The old manor house was surmounted by a battlemented parapet on which had been a number of curious stone figures, representing the various heathen deities. Many of these have been preserved on the north wall of the castle.

The castle is built asymmetrically, with the south tower facing the Tyne, though the main entrance (another tower) faces west: a projecting wing lies to the east. The Clock Tower, on the north side, belongs to the original house.

(Over page.) The tall tower with the arched doorway and large tripartite window, which is the main entrance, on the west side, to the castle. John Dobson was very proud of it and considered it his best work. Lyall Wilkes tells us that, at Beaufront, there is still William Cuthbert's account book, showing the names of the workmen concerned in the building of the house, the work they did and the amounts each received.

The only two amounts shown for Dobson's fees, as architect, total a modest two hundred and fifty pounds – far less than some of the craftsmen received!

Beaufront Castle, Hexham

John Dobson designed The Hags, a Tudor-style house, for Charles Head, in 1843.
The house, like so many others now, is divided into three parts – the main part of the building, the south wing and the mews.

Two-storeyed with seven-bays, the central three-bay section has an open pediment (within which is a semi-circular, sash window) and pedimented windows: the house also has a hipped roof and balustrade. It is first mentioned more than five centuries ago, in 1496. It is also believed that St John of Beverley lived on this site in the seventh century. In 1689, the house was owned by the Cotesworth family of Gateshead. Michael Cotesworth lived here from 1741-54 and he it was who rebuilt the south front (featured), "of white freestone and hewn-work", and so the building, as a whole, dates from this period.

The Jurin family became the owners in 1754 and they, too, made alterations to the house. Cotesworth altered the front, Jurin the north face and the offices. The 1769 edition of Antiquities of Northumberland, claim that the house is indebted to Jurin for "its present genteel appearance".

It passed into the hands of the Hunters of Medomsley, in County Durham, in the late 1780s and eventually to the Allgoods of Nunwick (through marriage), the present owners.

It has been in their possession for the best part of two hundred years.

John Dobson made alterations to the Hermitage, for R L Allgood Esq., in 1819.

The Reverend Thomas Andrews was lecturer at Hexham Abbey, from 1717-57, and he it was who built the house in gardens purchased from Mrs Dorothy Shaftoe. The original house was of five bays and had narrow windows but it was much smaller than the present building.

In 1757, the house passed to Thomas' brother, Robert, and in 1764 it passed again to Robert's daughter, Honour, who had married the Reverend Robert Clarke – also a lecturer at the Abbey.

Robert Clarke made a number of additions and alterations to the house. He added the third storey, the porch (on square pillars) facing the garden and both the east and west wings. The house was occupied by the Reverend Canon Barker (another lecturer) until the late 19th century. In 1915, a Miss Illingworth moved her school here from Scarborough, when that town was bombarded by the Germans. In 1918, the house was bought by a Mr Tully until, eventually, in 1926, it was sold to Hexham Urban Council, for use as a public library. Three years later the gardens were turned into a public park and bowling green.

The house is now used as offices by Tynedale Council.

The building on the right, masked in foliage, is a 19th century addition.

Hexham House, according to Pevsner, was altered by John Dobson, in 1819, for T R Beaumont.

The Leazes is situated one mile west of the busy market town of Hexham. The word Leazes means "the meadow". Locally, however, it has two other names; Myln Care (because of the road that once passed the Leazes to some old Chimney Mills) and Blind Man's Leaning (because an old beggar was reputed to have sat frequently outside the house).

John Dobson redesigned Leazes for a landed gentry family on a scale which created an impressive piece of architecture, which blended into its environment.

John Drayton (architect) said that mansions of Dobson's design were always considered an element in that environment and not an isolated piece of architecture.

In 1842, the Leazes was bought by James Gibson, one of the wealthiest landowners in the area, who subsequently changes his name to Kirsopp. Oddly enough, James Kirsopp never lived at the Leazes: it was never more than a building on land that he owned.

The 'bay' at the left of the building and the windows above were later additions to Dobson's house.

Here, as in other Dobson houses, the drainpipes and plumbing were installed internally so that no sight of them showed on the outer face of the building. In recent conversions to the Leazes this has had to be altered to meet current standards and the new plumbing and drainage had to be installed on existing structures.

In 1851, William Kirsopp bought the Leazes. He commissioned John Dobson to carry out extensive alterations to the house. A comprehensive rebuilding and enlargement programme began under the supervision of the Newcastle architect.

The date of the construction of the earlier part of the Leazes is unknown, as are the names of the architects and builders.

The earliest document concerning work done on the house dates from 1851, when a letter asked Dobson to alter and enlarge the house.

The earliest and, so far only, plans located are of the stables, piggeries, cart sheds and byres, and these are dated 1905. Examination of these plans will reveal the first size and shape of the house: plans for proposed buildings did not require planning permission before 1880. It is, however, reasonably possible to speculate on the date of the original construction of the Leazes by referring to other houses in the area, built of the same stone and with a known date of construction. This may have been 1840, more than ten years before its reconstruction. The alterations were extensive; more than three quarters of the house was rebuilt.

Nikolaus Pevsner, rather unkindly, describes the Leazes as, "not one of Dobson's better efforts".

The vagaries of the weather were always an important consideration in Dobson's thinking and planning and protection from the cold north wind was always a priority. In the case of the Leazes, he built the main entrance on the south-east corner, sheltered both from the north wind and the prevailing westerlies. The passage of cold currents of air (draughts!) is further restricted by the addition of a porch, at the main entrance, and then by double doors and passageway throughout. According to Dobson, this was to 'trap the air'. Dampness below the floors was overcome by placing a vent in the wall on a level with the surface of the ground, which allowed a thorough ventilation throughout the building. After adopting this plan, he apparently never knew an instance of 'dry rot'. This vent has also been called a 'dry drain' and has now become a common and expedient feature of building work. Yet this somewhat small 'discovery' by Dobson, was considered an extremely important 'invention' at the time. His assiduous attention to small detail was commendable, but then as Dobson himself said: "We build houses to live in and not just to look at: we need to do our utmost to encourage the useful, as the beautiful will take care of itself". Dobson's external elevations for the Leazes show a segmented front, divided into three narrow faces, across the top of which are triangular pediments, successfully exaggerating the height of the building. Another factor designed to give the impression of height is the actual design of the windows. John Dobson, like other of his contemporaries, appreciated the importance and dignity created by over-tall windows; their height being in the order of three times their width. The surrounding of the window is plain and clean-cut, designed to enhance their simplicity. The bay windows (in the west wing, for example) are also a regular feature of Dobson's country houses, their primary purpose being to afford panoramic, and often breathtaking views of the surrounding countryside. Nothing was allowed to interfere with the purity of Dobson's designs for country houses.

Built by John Dobson, between 1843 and 1845, for Sir Rowland Errington, "with spiky pinnacles on the corners and gables and a delightful porch with scrolly gable and little Jacobean arcades…"

A writer in the Hexham Courant, sometime before 1886, described the house as, "a quaint, queer-looking building in which the Elizabethan style of architecture prevails. Though the house has little to recommend it, in its character as a gentleman's mansion, the situation is rather a charming one".

Pevsner also believes the house is not one of Dobson's best, though he, to, does commend the porch.

John Dobson designed the Tudor-style Keeper's Cottage and Directors' Rooms, for Whittle Dean Water Company, in 1848.

The small Keeper's cottage, with its stepped gable and sets of tripartite windows is on the left (top picture). The more imposing Directors' Meeting Rooms are on the right.

This octagonal tower with the large windows designed by John Dobson, in 1848, was the Directors' Meeting Room.

Whittle Dean reservoirs consist of a group of four, the earliest major works of the Whittle Dean Water Company – later absorbed into the Newcastle and Gateshead Water Company.

The first three were designed in 1846 and completed in 1848. John Dobson added the fourth reservoir (below) in 1850.

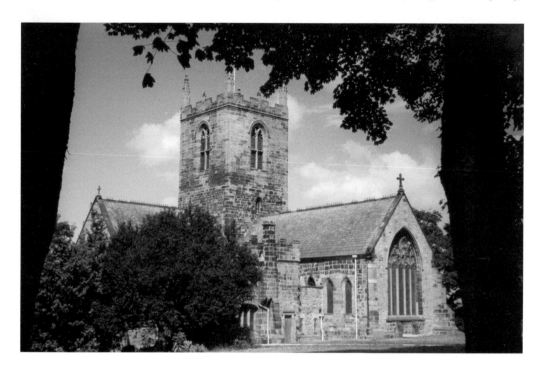

Margaret Jane Dobson, in her Memoir of 1885, gives the following detailed account of the restoration work her father carried out at St Michael's Church, in 1859:

"As another proof of Mr Dobson's inventive skill, the work that he did at the fine old Norman church of St Michael's … may be cited.

About the year 1828, a tower to contain a peal of six bells had been added, which weighed about 1,500 tons. This enormous mass of masonry caused the pillars on the north-east and south-east of the tower to shrink, as they had not originally been constructed to carry such pressure, added to which the foundations also were becoming seriously weakened by the formation of vaults.

In 1859, Mr Dobson undertook the arduous and difficult task of taking out the pillars and replacing them with new ones. This he ingeniously accomplished by carrying the solid mass of the super-incumbent masonry on wooden centres; and to make the work more secure he had the whole of the debris, within the tower, taken out to the depth of the foundations, and the space solidly filled in with concrete, above the foundations. The whole of this work was accomplished without any shrinking or settlement of the structure."

We are told by Mr J W A Robinson, who was a Churchwarden at the time, that "Mr Dobson with his usual literality, presented his professional fee towards the church restoration fund".

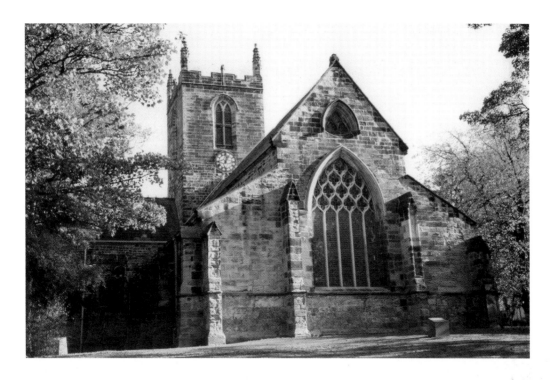

A Norman church once existed on the site of the present building but most of the present church dates from the 13th century.

The big five-light west and east windows are 14th century and are in the Decorated style.

"There must have been a timber hall before the stone castle", suggests T H Rowland.

The house constructed in the reign of Henry III (in the 13ᵗʰ century) was a country gentleman's dwelling and not a castle. It may well have been a single-storeyed house and then another level added.

The conversion of the old hall-house into a castle was accomplished by Gerald Widdrington who sometime after the death of Adam Swinburne, the previous owner (who died c.1317), married one of the Swinburne daughters and thus came into possession of the 'hall'.

He built up the (five) arched recesses, filling them with masonry, and heightened the building so that it now had a second floor. Widdrington made other substantial improvements, yet preferred to live in their castle at Widdrington rather than in Haughton and in a relatively short period of time the castle at Haughton became 'sadly neglected'.

The restoration work, carried out by John Dobson, was in keeping with the castle's ancient structure.

Tomlinson tells us that the figure of the castle is that of a double square, with two parallel vaults of a simple construction running on the basement, from end to end.

The walls of the castle are some eight feet thick and, in one part, eleven feet thick. Five square turrets crown the whole structure.

In 1542 the castle was repaired after it was partly destroyed by Liddesdale raiders: John Dobson's restoration took place in 1845.

In 1844-5, John Dobson carried out substantial restoration work for William Smith. Smith, nicknamed 'the Buccaneer' (no doubt because his wealth came from his maritime adventures), moved the main entrance to the north front, enclosed the park and diverted the road. He also removed the old village and established a wall-garden.

In 1876, Anthony Salvin added the west wing (featured). As a result, the castle now consists of two distinct parts – the old, medieval, main building and the 'modern' west wing.

The unusual entrance on the east front.

Robert Hugill (Castles and Peles of the English Border) makes the following observation:

"It is hard to believe that towards the end of the 18th century Haughton was 'chiefly dismantled, some few apartments only remaining habitable', so well has it been rebuilt and restored … since then. Originally, it was a rugged 'tower house' with five square turrets … and a stout barmkin (now mostly gone)".

H L Honeyman believes Haughton "is the most interesting inhabited house in the county….".

This rather fine residential terrace has been attributed to John Dobson. First proposed
by him in 1820, it was finally built in 1838.

The wings and centre project slightly.

Jesmond Dene House   (Jesmond Dene road)

Known previously as Black Dene House, Jesmond Dene House was built in 1822, by architect John Dobson, for the physician Thomas Emerson Headlam, a one-time Mayor of Newcastle.

In 1871, the house was bought by Andrew (later Sir Andrew) Noble, a business partner of Lord (William) Armstrong.

Norman Shaw made alterations to the house, in 1875, and then, in 1896, the house was completely rebuilt by F W Rich: virtually nothing now remains of the earlier work.

Sir Andrew Noble died in 1915 but the house remained in the possession of the family until 1930 when it was bought by Newcastle City Council. Underground tunnels were constructed shortly before the Second World War.

In 1954, it became a residential school for girls with learning difficulties but, by the end of the 1990s, it had been abandoned by the Council and had fallen into disrepair.

Jesmond Dene House is now a luxury hotel.

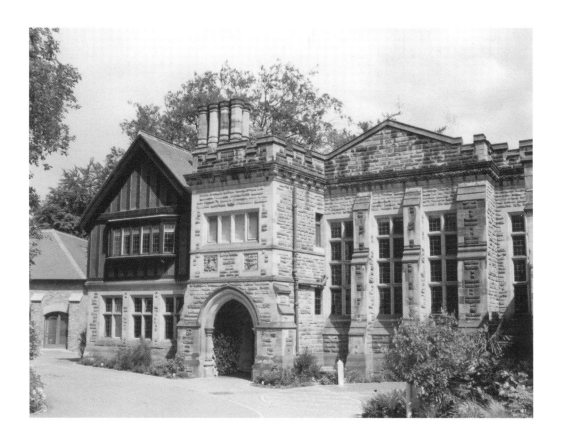

Jesmond Dene House – now a luxury hotel.

A Gothic house, built at the beginning of the 19th century (as West Jesmond House) and later added to in 1817 and between 1823-27 by architect John Dobson, for Sir Thomas Burdon.

Dobson's work, however, is now largely embedded in substantial later additions by Thomas Oliver Junior, in 1869, and later, in 1884 and 1895, by T R Spence.

The south front (above), including Dobson's work of 1823-27, is a "glorious confection of elaborately decorated battlements and gables, corner towers and richly traceried windows".

The main entrance on the south side.

Bought in 1870 by Lord William Armstrong's partners, Charles Mitchell, from 1946 until its closure in 2008 Jesmond Towers was the La Sagesse Roman Catholic Convent High School.

The north side of the building, overlooking Jesmond Dene, is much plainer and less ornate than the more impressive south front, with its wide, unaffected windows and solid, octagonal, corner turrets: it represents the earlier house.

Originally, it had a high terrace hiding the basement and was only of three floors: the fourth floor was added by Thomas Oliver Junior.

John Dobson designed Nazareth House (previously known both as Villa Reale and Sandyford Park) for one Captain Dutton, in 1817.

"The exterior is enlivened with a perhaps over-large Doric portico on the entrance front and a large bay on the garden front."

John Dobson designed the Cemetery Gates and was responsible for the laying out of the entire cemetery. The north entrance consists of two ashlar chapels with Doric pilasters and turrets.

J C Loudon (1783-1843), horticultural writer and architect, born in Cambuslang, Strathclyde and a major influence in London landscape and domestic architecture, who published several of Dobson's designs and who became an authority on cemetery design, greatly admired Dobson's entrance.

Lowdon wrote: "It was the most appropriate cemetery lodge that he knew because it could never be mistaken for an entrance to a public park or a country residence."

The Builder, of January 14th, 1865, commented: "The laying out of the new cemetery at Jesmond, Newcastle (in 1834), afforded Mr Dobson scope for the display of his ability both as an architect and a landscape gardener and the result is well worthy the attention of the student as an excellent example."

"The handsome chapels and (north) entrance gate of Jesmond Cemetery were the result of his skill" (The Newcastle Daily Journal of the 9th of January, 1865).

The south entrance: the two massive, gate piers.

Jesmond Parish Church, Eskdale , Terrace, Jesmond.

A late, Early English Church, with a big, pinnacle tower; designed by John Dobson (1857-61), and built in memory of Richard Clayton.

It is also known as the Clayton Memorial Church.

149

The memorial to Archibald Reed; Sheriff, Alderman and six times Mayor of Newcastle, who died in 1842, is built of sandstone ashlar.

The huge, two-stage Gothic tower has pinnacled diagonal buttresses and an octagonal spire.

Designed by John Dobson (in 1843) and actually signed by him, the monument is now (2008) in a very sorry condition and in some danger of collapse. Indeed, it is overgrown to such an extent the spire is hardly visible any more.

Albert Silvertop bought the land at Minsteracres in 1725, but it was George Silvertop, while living in Stella, who built up the family's fortune in the coal trade, with shares in mines at Greenside, Winlaton and Blaydon – and it was he who added most of the land to the estate. His son John built the present mansion, between 1780 and 1800, on the site of an earlier house of which nothing now remains except, perhaps, the lodges and the stables.

Tomlinson writes that, "The Hall is a fine stately building and was improved and enlarged (in 1866-67) by the addition of a north wing." Elsewhere it is described as "a large, informal house".

Successive members of the family lived at Minsteracres until, in 1952, Charles sold the house and the adjoining parkland to a religious order – the Passionists.

Minsteracres had finally, after more than a century and a half, passed out of the hands of the Silvertop family.

John Dobson made large additions to the house, in 1816, for George Silvertop: these are believed to include the large bay-window (centre) and the colonnade (to the right of the tree).

The north front.

A Roman Catholic chapel, in the Gothic style, and dedicated to Saint Elizabeth, was added in 1852-54, to replace an oratory. This small chapel was built on the instructions of Henry Silvertop – who had changed his name from Englefield. His wife, Eliza, laid the foundation stone in September, 1852, and the church was dedicated by the Bishop of Hexham on August 24th, 1854.

In 601, Pope Gregory sent a Roman monk named Paulinus to assist Augustine's mission in Kent.   In 625, King Edwin of Northumbria married the Princess Ethelburga, a daughter of the King of Kent, and she and Paulinus travelled north to live in the royal residence at Ad-Gefrin, less than a mile to the east of the present church.

Edwin embraced the Christian faith in 627 and his fellow Northumbrians, eager to follow their sovereign's example, were baptised in the nearby River Glen.

The first recorded incumbent of St Gregory's is one Stephen, who was priest here from 1153 until 1197. Very little remains of his ancient church and over the passing centuries the building has known a chequered history; indeed, there were several periods when the church was a complete ruin.

The chancel is a very remarkable one, being, it is supposed, the vaulted chamber of a pele or store house built out of the ruins of the Norman church. Built up in the wall of the tower on the outside is a child's coffin lid with a floriated cross upon it.

Attached to the wall behind the reading desk is a curious piece of sculpture representing the Virgin and the Magi – the Wise Men appear, incongruously, in kilts!

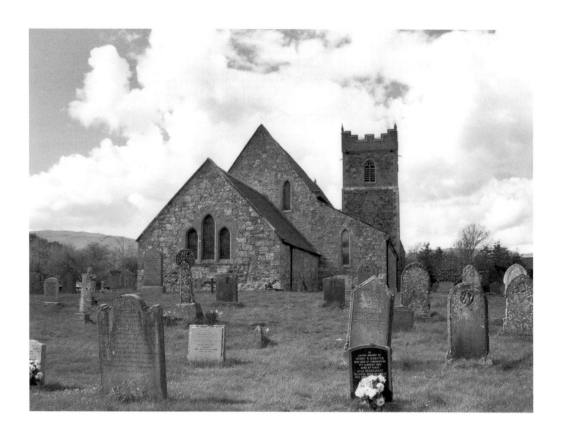

A place of Christian worship has stood on this site since at least the eleventh century.

How many times the church has been rebuilt is uncertain.

The last major restoration, undertaken by John Dobson was in 1856. He produced the nave, the porch and the north aisle, in lancet style, so typical of much of his work.

This restoration was completed in 1860 and some years later the perpendicular style tower was added.

A small, two-storeyed mansion of c.1820; three bays wide, 'built on the site of an earlier farm' (the remains of which can be seen on the right of the main building), and attributed to John Dobson 'on grounds of style'. The centre section of the south face projects slightly and the entrance is via a square porch with arched doorway, which may have been added later.

Longhirst Hall   (Longhirst)

Longhirst Hall was built for William Lawson, from designs by the architect John Dobson, between 1824-28 when, it is said, Dobson was producing the finest work of his career.

The Hall has rightly been described as one of his masterpieces. It is not a particularly large house but the attention to detail of its masonry, its carving and its general construction is said to be almost faultless.

The melodramatic entrance front, on the west side, is dominated by a great portico of two giant, fluted Corinthian columns the capitals of which were an original composition by the architect.

Longhirst Hall is believed to be Dobson's only design graced with a pediment.

156

Tomlinson described it as, "a mansion of fine grained and warm tinted sandstone…"
The Corinthian entablature, surmounted by a pediment, is continued all around the principal building.

The two-storeyed, five-bay south front features a large, three-bay, central bow, while the east front consists of a rank of five tall, evenly spaced windows.

Of Longhirst Hall it has been written that "in both its design and construction it is almost perfect".

John Grundy and Grace McCombie declare that, "It is not a large house but the entrance front is a splendid design, exciting and theatrical. It has a tightly compressed full-height Corinthian portico with a pediment, the only time Dobson used a pediment on any of his houses". Lyall Wilkes describes it as, "the most melodramatic front of all Dobson's houses".

Frank Graham asserts that, "The great Newcastle architect was then (1828) doing his finest work in the classical tradition and this villa is one of his masterpieces."

Charles William Bigge asked his close friend, Sir Charles Monck (above), to prepare designs for a large mansion to be built within his estate (on part of the 2,900 acres of land he had purchased from the Earl of Carlisle, in 1808).

It is thought three different designs were prepared before arriving at the final choice.

Charles Lambert Monck (1779-1867) was born Charles Lambert Middleton but changed his name to Monck at the behest of his maternal grandfather and, while supervising the building of Linden Hall, he was elected to parliament to represent Northumberland.

Monck was an ardent Greek Revivalist and Linden Hall (which Bigge named after the nearby Linden Burn) shows strong examples of this style, in the four heavy, unfluted Doric columns of its portico, with its full entablature, frieze of triglyphs and metopse and cornice.

Monck supervised the construction of Linden Hall from the laying of its foundation stone, on July 30th, 1810, until its completion in 1812 and final occupation in 1813. Bigge's entry in his diary for June 8th, 1813, reads ".... to Linden, where for the first time I slept in my own house".

It is believed John Dobson collaborated with Monck in the designing of the Hall, after having returned, in 1811, from serving his apprenticeship and a

further year in London, studying with John Varley. He was asked by Sir Charles to detail the portico and the windows. Indeed, until fairly recently, it was widely believed that Linden Hall was a purely John Dobson house. Pevsner, for example, in his 1957 edition of The Buildings of England: Northumberland, described it as, "an early Dobson house". Frank Graham states, "This elegant house by Dobson was built in 1812-13, for Charles William Bigge." Bruce Allsopp, however, has discovered that the house was, in fact, designed by Sir Charles Monck and that Dobson's contribution, important though it was, was far less than he had previously been given credit for. Lyall Wilkes makes the point that, "... had the new known date of Linden (1812) have been known previously, more hesitation in the attribution to Dobson might have been shown since so important and large a commission would not readily have been given to a young architect in the first year of his practice". Linden Hall was built of local stone quarried from Horsley Common, south of Longhorsley, and Monck was credited with having employed some of the finest stonemasons in the country.

In 1903, the Hall was purchased by Laurence William Adamson JP. The Adamson family lived her for sixty years and during that time were looked after by a full complement of staff. During their period of residence, the Hall was maintained as an auxiliary hospital for sick and wounded soldiers from the First World War... between March 1916 and April 1919. After the death of Miss Muriel Adamson the Hall and its contents were sold. It was purchased by Mr John M Liddell, who lived there until 1978, when the entire estate was bought by Callers-Pegasus Travel Service Ltd. It is now owned by Macdonald's.

The six-bay east front.

The nine-bay south front.

Mitford is a larger version of Prestwick and was designed in 1823 for Bertram Osbaldeston Mitford ' but building was delayed, perhaps because of the impending marriage of the owner, until 1828-9'.

The site is typically Dobsonian, designed to give the optimum view – the drawing room windows looking down on the River Wansbeck, to Mitford Church and to the massive castle mound crowned by the Mitford's first home, Mitford Castle.

Hodgson describes the Hall as "a very handsome square edifice: the beautiful white sandstone, of which its outer walls are built, is obtained from a stratum of rock which forms the bed of the (River) Font".

Mitford Hall: an ashlar, two-storeyed, three-bay villa with a Greek Doric porch and balustrade, designed by John Dobson (1823-28).

The east front has five bays. The wide, recessed central section contains three windows set unusually close together.

The central section of the longer north-east wing was demolished in 1970, but its tower-like end section is complete, as is the attached conservatory with Tuscan pilasters.

Mitford and Meldon Park have strikingly similar, Italianate stable-block towers. "Typical Dobson", says Pevsner, "with a cupola on a ridge".

All Saints Church   (Monkwearmouth, Sunderland)

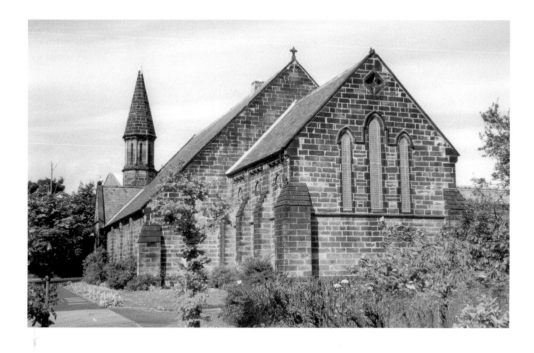

A church by John Dobson: 1845-49. It is small, in the Early English style and, as one writer puts it, "an excellent effect is achieved by simple means".

The Chantry   (Morpeth)

The Chantry was founded in the 13th century, for its priest to say Mass, pray for all Christian souls, and to keep a Grammar School. Edward VI granted the school a charter in 1552 and it remained in the building until 1846. Thereafter the building has been used as a cholera hospital, a mineral water factory and even as a public convenience. It was restored in the 1980s and is now a Tourist Information Centre, a Craft Centre a Bagpipe Museum and a Local History Museum.

(Top); the east end has twin gables each with a pair of heavily arched windows and each of which has a single, oval window above.
(Right); the west end is fairly complete. It has a pointed arched doorway in a 'multi-moulded surround, with two, double-chamfered windows above, and a bell-cote.

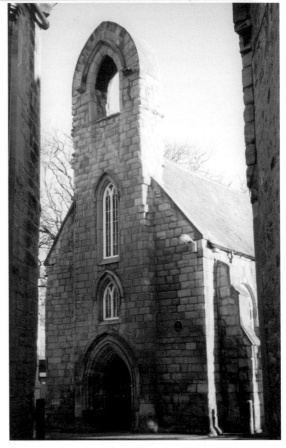

The building was repaired by John Dobson, in 1827.

167

The 'New Gaol' was situated on the south side of the River Wansbeck and on the east side of the road leading down from the Railway Station into the town centre.

The Act of Parliament required for the building of it was passed in March, 1821 and plans for it advertised in June of that same year.   John Dobson was the successful candidate in a competition to design the Gaol, a House of Correction and a Sessions House.

Dobson claimed his winning design was inspired by the castles he had seen and studied at Conway, Beaumarie and Caernarvon, in North Wales. The 'New Gaol' was actually constructed between 1822-28, and was equivalent in size, scale and cost, to its Newcastle counterpart. The masons employed to do the building were Messrs. King, Kyle and Hall. The building in the photograph (the Court or Sessions House) was originally the castellated Gateway to the 'New Gaol'.

An imposing structure, seventy-two feet high: on the ground floor it had, in front, on the south side, the porters lodge and on the north a grand stone staircase leading to the Sessions House and other apartments above. Behind, on the ground floor, were the chapel, on the right, and the sick wards and bath, on the left.

On the second floor of the Gateway was the Sessions House or Hall, for county meetings.... ninety-two feet by sixty-four feet and forty-one feet high. It was a heptagonal semi-circle surrounded by a gallery large enough to hold 3,500 persons and had under it rooms for the Clerk of the Peace, Counsel and Petty Jury members and cells for prisoners on trial, beside a passage and lobbies for witnesses.

The Court House is often understandably mistaken, by strangers to the town, for Morpeth Castle which, in fact, stands on a hill opposite, overlooking Carlisle Park.

Full descriptions of the three Morpeth bridges – the High Ford Bridge, the Low Ford Bridge and the 'New Bridge' – and the circumstances and events leading up to their construction can be found in the 2000/02 editions of Dobson on Dobson. In order to accommodate new material I have decided not to repeat these in this present edition.

Anyone wishing to read more about the bridges – particularly the 'New Bridge' – can easily consult either of the previous books which, although out of print, can be found in local libraries.

High Ford Bridge ' was built by public subscription and under the inspection of the County Surveyor'. Designed by John Dobson and built between 1828-30 it crosses the River Wansbeck at High Ford, on the Mitford Road.
It is a handsome structure of two arches and the stone for its construction came from Morpeth quarry.

The bridge crosses the River Wansbeck on the road between Morpeth and Mitford. It is described as 'plain and simple' by John Dobson, it was built in 1836.

The 'New Bridge' (the Telford Bridge)   (Morpeth)

In the 2000 edition of "Dobson on Dobson" I have set out, at some length, the arguments over who designed the 'New Bridge' in Morpeth, John Dobson or Thomas Telford, and it is not my intention to reproduce them here. In 1832, the Reverend John Hodgson published his 'A History of Morpeth'. The significance of this date is crucial to the argument since the book was published within one year of the opening of the 'New Bridge'.

Hodgson writes: "Morpeth 'New Bridge' is now building (April, 1831) at a short distance below the old one, between the chapel and the mill; and under the authority of an act for that purpose, which received the royal assent, June 1st, 1829.

Mr Telford chose or approved the site on which is the bridge is built and the designs for it, which were finally adopted, are by Mr Dobson, architect of Newcastle."

It is universally recognised that John Hodgson was a man of great wisdom, integrity and perspicacity, highly intelligent and of an unusual enquiring nature, with a wide and lively interest in all manner of subjects. It seems unlikely, therefore, that, writing this history of the town with which he was so closely associated, and at the time he did (1831), his information would be inaccurate, for so much of the other detail is correct in every particular. He had, after all, no personal axe to grind on behalf of John Dobson, nor any quarrel with Thomas Telford. It seems inconceivable and entirely out of character that he should make any claim for Dobson's involvement if such a claim was erroneous. Equally, it is remarkable (writing at the very time of the bridge's construction, when public interest was at its peak and information so readily available for public scrutiny) that his statement should be so seemingly at odds with the correspondence of Morpeth solicitor, William Woodman (born March, 1806 and whose papers are now in the Northumberland County Records Office at Woodhorn), who makes no mention at all of Dobson's involvement.

Yet Hodgson's statement is both clear and unequivocal: "… the designs for the bridge, which were finally accepted, are by Mr Dobson".

I am by no means alone in believing that the credit for the design of Morpeth's 'New Bridge' rightfully belongs to John Dobson: a number of other writers, whose opinions I value, share this belief.

From the information available – bearing in mind we are dealing with a period of time generally notorious for its inaccuracy and poor, often non-existent written records, and that such information as is available is of a fragmented and sketchy nature, with many pieces of the 'jigsaw' missing, it seems reasonable to conclude that:-

(a) the engineer, Thomas Telford, chose the site for the bridge (… this is generally accepted with evidence to support the assumption.
(b) Thomas King and William Beldon were the contractors who actually built the bridge (… proof for this assertion is to be found on the two stone tablets inlaid on the walls on either side of the bridge).
(c) The architect John Dobson designed the bridge.

The evidence to support this latter claim is found in the testimony of the Reverend John Hodgson, writing at the time of the bridge's actual construction. It is unimaginable to believe that Hodgson would make this contention if it were not true.

The bridge consists of three arches; the middle one of fifty feet and the two side ones each have a span of forty feet. The centre arch rises sixteen feet above the river and the other two thirteen feet each. The stone for the building of the bridge was brought, by rail, from Netherton.

Variously described as one of the finest of Dobson's early classical houses, though it was not a new house but an earlier Queen Anne house which John Dobson redesigned in 1825, re-fronting the original house and adding projecting wings.

The fine 'bow' to the west of the Garden Front, which Frank Graham believes "… helps to shape one of the finest rooms of the house".

The original Queen Anne house stands in the centre of the south front. To this Dobson added the lower projecting wings. To the two-and-a-half storey, five-bay centre he added an open gallery or colonnade, supported by four Ionic columns. The top of the house has a fine honeysuckle frieze. The wings have full-length tripartite windows while those above are only half the size. To the west he rounded off this fascinating façade with a fine bow-window.

The entrance front on the east side of the house.

"The entrance front has two storeys and five broad bays: the centre and outer bay break forward slightly.

In the centre bay there is a large Ionic porte cochère with two columns, in antis, set against a loggia of three pairs of Ionic columns, which spans the centre three bays. There is a cornice and parapet with panels, carved with scrolls, palmettes and anthemia. The Hall has a hipped roof".
(Ref. Country Life magazine: February 17th, 1966).

The beautiful Ionic porte cochère, which forms the entrance to the Hall on the east side.

Nunnykirk Hall is now the property of Northumberland County Council and is a school for dyslexic children.

Described by Pevsner as, "an early (John) Dobson house, with a five-bay ashlar front and doorway with a broad, radial fanlight under a round-arched recess".

The house was built in 1812, for the Reverend Henry Wastell. Its late owner, Mr William Arthur Benson, was able to give me the following additional information, relating to the house and its history. The Reverend Wastell and his wife had two daughters, one of whom died while the other married one of the younger sons of the Coulson family of Blenkinsopp. William Benson's father also married into the Coulson family and he subsequently bought Newbrough Hall c.1901.

William was born here in 1905 and lived here his entire life (he being ninety-two years old when we had this conversation), except for the time he spent in military service, when he rose to the rank of Major. After he acquired the Hall, William's father employed the services of an Edinburgh architect called Deas (in 1902), who made substantial, internal alterations to the house and who also installed the drawing room bay window … otherwise, the outside of the building has not altered from the time it was built: it still remains a two-storeyed, five-bay stone house with projected pedimented centre, with steps leading up to an arched doorway.

The original building (Newton Hall) is dated 1811.

W H Blackett commissioned John Dobson to carry out additions and alterations in 1851.

The south front had five bays; the pedimented centrepiece was added later.

Since the end of the last war, the Hall has been adapted for use as a school and it is now Mowden Hall School, Newton, near Stocksfield.

Mike Kirkup, in his splendid book, Was there ever Railway Row? A History of North Seaton Colliery and Village (published by Woodhorn Press, Newbiggin by the Sea), gives the following information about the Hall and its adjoining Watch Tower:-

"North Seaton Hall, with its adjacent Watch Tower, was built by the famous north-east architect, John Dobson, whose name is commemorated in one of Newcastle's city streets. It was initially the property of wealthy William Watson, who owned most of the land around North Seaton in the early 1800s. It was eventually bought by the Ashington Coal Company and became the residence of Edmund O Southern, an agent for the Company. By the late 1920s we find the Hall being used "to train young lads about to emigrate to Australia, Canada and New Zealand in the art of farming".

The Hall saw service in the Second World War as a billet for soldiers and several wooden huts were built in the grounds to accommodate prisoners of war.

Upon nationalisation, in 1947, the Hall became the property of the National Coal Board. It was soon housing what we would term today 'one-parent families' and others whose social behaviour was somewhat unacceptable.

Like most of the area's fine old buildings, North Seaton Hall was allowed to fall into a state of disrepair and it was eventually demolished in 1960".

My thanks to Mike Kirkup for permitting me to reproduce this article.

Lyall Wilkes (John 'Dobson, Architect and landscape Gardener) raises the following point:-

"It is not known, beyond doubt, which was Dobson's first building, Mackenzie is History of Newcastle (1827) states that the Royal Jubilee School…was built between 1810-11, from Dobson's designs; and if this is true then it must be Dobson's first building.

It was also listed in the obituary notice in the Newcastle Daily Journal of January 9th, 1865, but it is not listed in Margaret Jane Dobson's list of her father's buildings (in her Memoir of 1885), who gives her father's first building as North Seaton Hall, and the date as 1813. Margaret Jane's Memoir is often the subject of criticism: its inaccuracies are said to consist of claiming work for her father that was not his. It is difficult to believe (says Wilkes) that John Dobson did not tell his daughter, which was his first building, so if it was the Royal Jubilee School, why is it not on her list?

The Baptist Church   (Howard Street, North Shields)

John Dobson's church of 1846 has three central windows above a moulded arch door. The gable is buttressed. Pevsner says the style is Romanesque the Newcastle Daily Journal described it as neo-Norman.

John Dobson was born here on the 9th of December, 1787
*Note the error (below) in the date of Dobson' death.

The Presbyterian Church of St Columba   (North Shields)

Designed by John Dobson (1856-7) and built in the Palladian style. It has five arched bays with Tuscan half columns.
St Columba's is now a United Reform Church.

The Scottish Presbyterian Church   (Howard Street, North Shields)

The church, now a Salvation Army Hall, has been variously described as 'bold', 'unsophisticated', 'naïve' and 'crude' in both its design and its appearance. Known as the 'Scotch Church' and built in 1811; it was designed by John Dobson.

Standing as it does, on Howard Street (Saville Street to the right), this building – designed by John Dobson (1844-45) – originally included police offices, a museum, savings bank and the Mechanics Institute: it is now Council Offices and a Magistrates' Court.

The Church of St John the Evangelist   (Otterburn)

Tomlinson tells us that the church, built after designs by John Dobson and dedicated to St John the Evangelist, was opened in 1857.

It is a handsome stone building, in the Decorated style, with a large geometrical east window.

Though small by comparison to others designed by John Dobson, Prestwick Lodge is considered to be among the very best of Dobson's early houses. The stonework at Prestwick is quite superb. Quite apart from the beautifully cut blocks of sandstone with which the house is built, the mortar layer between the stones is so fine you can hardly see it. This is a fine compliment to the masons employed by John Dobson – the standard of their workmanship is almost perfect.

The Tyneside Classical Tradition makes the following observations:- "Dobson's best early work, such as Prestwick Lodge (of 1815), is simple and straightforward; late Georgian houses, often with nothing more than a Tuscan or Doric porch, for external emphasis, and a few classical details inside".

The main entrance doorway, with its broad Tuscan pilasters.

Since Mike and Kim Wilson bought Prestwick Lodge, in 1979, they have carried out an ongoing programme of restoration.

The original main entrances door (Dobson's) was of soft wood; they have faithfully reproduced and replaced this with hardwood.

In all other respects it is identical.

The 'bath-house' (also of 1815) was part of the service wing. It is some fourteen and a half feet long and ten feet wide. In one corner, and in addition to the internal dimensions of the room, is a kind of vestibule (which Mr Wilson believes may have been a small 'steam room'), measuring six feet by six, which at one time contained seats. The actual bath (built of stone believed to have come from Belsay and lined, thinly, with lead to prevent leakage) is eight feet long and six feet wide. The 'pool' is five feet deep and has seven stone steps leading down into the water.

Small statues on the window ledges create the ambience of an ancient Roman bath-house.

Lancelot 'Capability' Brown (1715-83), the renowned Northumbrian landscape gardener, believed that in a garden which was protected from the north and east winds a man might grow 'almost anything'. This superb garden wall at Prestwick, designed by John Dobson, has a form of boiler heating arrangement, at either end of the wall, from which warm air is induced, through ducts, between the outer skins of the wall. Every so often, along the wall, to protect the fruit trees from the hard winter frosts. The coping stones along the top of the wall were an additional protection from the wind's down draught.

The east front.

The west front.

The east front of the Hall, with its crenellated wings and mullioned windows, was burned down on May 15th, 1752. It was finally restored, after more than sixty years, by architect John Dobson, in 1819.

In 1819 John Dobson also added two battlemented, octagonal 'wings' to the existing pele tower.

The Bosanquet family believe the pele was founded in the reign of King Stephen, at the beginning of the twelfth century and was both altered and enlarged during the reign of the first Queen Elizabeth.

On a promontory called Guile Point, at the northern extremity of Ross Sands on the north Northumberland coast) south of, and immediately opposite, the harbour of the island of Lindisfarne, there stands two tall slender, tapering 'pyramids' of red sandstone ashlar.   These two obelisks stand in an east/west line and are some five hundred feet apart.

These beacons, brick built and on a sandstone base, were built by John Dobson, in 1820, for Trinity House.   The east beacon (which is sixty-seven feet high) cost £135 to construct: its west neighbour is some eighty-three feet high and cost £186.

Inside the redbrick 'shell' are the original timber beacons, still in surprisingly good condition.   Around 1930, however, the west beacon was struck by lightening and its upper timbers are now charred.

The beacons, which are listed, were last renovated in 1992.

On one face of the westernmost beacon is a stone tablet on which is inscribed "Repaired 1916: Capt. E W Kent, master: Capt. J C Hardy, Deputy".

There is another tablet, on a different face of the same beacon, which reads "Restored 1937: Capt. Brown, Master: Capt. Hardy, Deputy".

Described as "one of the most endearing of all Gothic houses in Count Durham…. It is the epitome of the late 18th century house, at its most genial and charming".

In 1762, Sir John Swinburne created the house substantially as we see it today, a medium-sized house representing a happy amalgam of Georgian and Gothic features. Yet, the Gothic features are minimal: the form of the upper windows and the fanciful bay-window, with its "pretty pattern of glazing bars". This is really, suggests Neville Whittaker, Gothic fashion applied as decoration only, to the simple form of a Georgian house. On the death of Sir John Swinburne the house and estate passed to his brother Henry, a man of great taste and, as an indefatigable traveller, of great experience. So perhaps it was natural he should select the fashionable Gothic style for the improvement of his house which, basically, is a simple rectangle.

The pinnacle (centre of picture) is from the old Houses of Parliament: the cupola (extreme right) is from the demolished mansion of Beaudesert, in Staffordshire.

In 1815, John Dobson made alterations to the Hall, for R S Surtees: both a corn mill on the estate (1819) and the Handley Cross Bridge (1815) are also believed to be the work of John Dobson.

Different writers, over the years, have expressed their colourful and critical opinions and descriptions of Sir John Vanburgh's impressive creation; some flattering others not quite so. One describes it as, "the most important 18th century country house in the North-East of England". He adds: "a superb but impractical house". Another eulogises – "A grand piece of architectural theatre", adding; "a masterpiece of architectural imagination". Pevsner describes it as, "a sombre house of smoke-blackened stone, facing a bleak scene, with the smoke of Blyth and the sea in the distance to the north". In a more kindly vein, however, he continues; "no other Vanburgh house is so mature, so compact and so powerful… for though it belongs to the hand of its master, in every detail, it is yet completely individual with its own composition and mood".

Seaton Delaval Hall was built between 1718 and 1728, for Admiral George Delaval. Vanburgh was more than fifty years old when he designed the house; the admiral was older and both were dead before its completion. The architectural details of the Hall are classical and the general plan, a square central block with arcaded wings running at right angles to it, is that of a Palladio villa, but the central block itself, "with its dramatically jagged silhouette and octagonal corner towers", has more in common with a medieval castle…

The centre block is one of the most uncompromising and original pieces of design of the period and the two long stable and domestic wings enclose a courtyard that suggests nothing as much as a "stage set". The Hall was "seriously marred" (one critic complained), c.1770, by the addition of a large wing extending the south elevation, seven bays to the east. John Dobson proposed to rebuild the east wing "to conform closely with Vanburgh's architectural detailing", with octagonal corner towers repeating, exactly, those on the central block. Dobson also proposed the building of a matching west wing which would have created an enormous south front of twenty-three bays. The owner, Sir Jacob Henry Astley, apparently found John Dobson's proposals unacceptable and his successor seems not to have been much interested in Dobson's plans.

In a letter I received from Mr F Hetherington (sub-agent of the Delaval Estate since 1946!), in October 1997, he wrote:- "… there are (now) no signs of John Dobson's work on exterior photographs". "Dobson came here," he continues, "in *1818, and made plans for a grand restoration of the centre part of the hall, which were not acceptable to the then-owner, Sir Jacob Astley." Mr Hetherington is slightly in error here since Sir Jacob Died on the 28 April, 1817: Dobson must, therefore, have proposed his plan to Sir Jacob early in 1817, or possibly in 1816, but certainly not in 1818. However, Mr Hetherington goes on: "The (second) fire occurred on the 22 January, 1822, following which John Dobson was commissioned to make the house both wind and watertight; the main works being new roofs with timbers, on the east and west wings of the centre. He also strengthened the south with iron columns to replace the stone ones and by building brick arches".

I am immensely grateful to Mr Hetherington (and his daughter), who, sadly, passed away in the year 2000, aged 90 years, both for his kind interest in supplying this information and through whose good offices I received Lord Hastings' permission to take my photographs of the Hall. The west wing of the Hall was burned down on May 6th, 1752, but rebuilt to the original plan. The second fire, referred to by Mr Hetherington, originated in a chimney and reduced the main building to a splendid ruin. Only the sterling efforts of the staff, both estate and domestic workers, saved the two wings. "The heat was so intense, "wrote W W Tomlinson "that the glass in the windows was reduced to a liquid state and the lead on the roof poured down like water".

It was not until 1860 that John Dobson was commissioned to re-roof the block destroyed in the second fire and thus, suggests Faulkner, "enabled the house's architectural glories to survive to the present day".

Seaton Delaval Hall has had a chequered, many would say, unlucky history. Twice badly burnt; the first time on May 6th, 1752 and again on January 22nd, 1822; left roofless for the best part of half a century: badly damaged by troops when it was requisitioned by the army in both World Wars. Had the house, thereafter, been denied the necessary, even vital maintenance and repair it was in danger not only of becoming derelict but (the present owner believes) it was in imminent danger of total collapse.

The magnificent south front, with its portico of detached, elegantly fluted Ionic columns carrying a balustraded balcony and the wide staircase leading up to the portico.

As a result of the splendid efforts, after 1945, made by Lord Hastings – including the re-roofing of both the east and west wings, the repair of the stables, the replacement of the ceilings and the restoration of various rooms, etc – the Hall was eventually opened to the public, in 1950.

The imposing north front "with its dramatically jagged silhouette and octagonal corner towers" has more in common with a medieval castle…. A flight of sixteen steps ascends to a lofty Doric portico whose superb columns, with their richly embellished entablatures, form a most commanding entrance. In the tympanum of the pediment above, the arms of the family and various trophies are carved.

The whole of the finely sculptured façade is crowned with a balustrade on which are arranged several elegant vases on pedestals.

The west front (left of picture) overlooks the gardens.
The south front portico is on the right.

The east front.

Two immense wings, with beautiful arcades running along the whole length of their fronts, enclose a spacious courtyard.

The east wing, containing the 'cathedral-like' stables and the west wing – containing the vast kitchen, and where, incidentally, the fire broke out in 1752, enclose a courtyard "that suggests nothing as much as a stage set".

To the east and west, at right-angles to the central building, are colonnades flanking the stables on one side and the kitchen ranges on the other… thus providing a courtyard.

The owner in 1998, Mr Colin Lawson, wrote to me as follows:-

"I confirm my best estimate (for the dating of the 'Parsonage House') of 1855-56, from the date of the invitation to tender (1855) and the inclusion of the 'Parsonage House' on the Ordnance Survey of 1858. The year 1848 was the year of the land conveyance and the start of construction of the Holy Trinity Church".

The building of the church was completed, in 1849, by John Green. Contemporary evidence points to the fact that the Vicarage was built in 1855 by John Dobson.

Flotterton House   (Snitter, near Rothbury)

A fine country house was built here for Christopher Weallands, overlooking the Coquet Valley and the Simonside Hills.

The house is not large: two-storeyed with five bays. The central, three-bay section on the garden (south) side is a 'bow'.

The house dates from 1823 and the architect was John Dobson.

The south front, overlooking the Coquet Valley.

The east front has three, twelve-pane, sash windows on the ground floor and three, nine-pane, sash windows on the first floor.

The Church of Saint Nicholas is a plain structure with an octagonal spire rising from a square tower. It was rebuilt and enlarged between 1799 and 1820.

The architect of Saint Nicholas' Church was John Dodds.

The present church is believed to have replaced a Saxon building.

In 1819 John Dobson added galleried north and south aisles. The south tower porch was added in 1833. The enlargement follows the same classical Georgian lines.

Before the Dissolution Cheeseburn belonged to Hexham Priory. In 1638, it was the seat of Thomas Widdrington Esq, whose son, Sir Thomas, became Recorder of York; Lard Keeper in 1647; Speaker to Parliament in 1656 and Lord Chief Baron in 1658.

From this family Cheeseburn, descended, by the female line, to Ralph Riddell.

The Widdringtons were very involved in the Jacobite Rebellion of 1715. One of the family, who owned the Grange before it eventually passed to the Riddells, Ralph Widdrington, was imprisoned and under sentence of death at Liverpool. He managed to escape with a servant from the gaol, by means of a rope. During the escape Ralph lost all his fingernails from one hand, clinging to the rope. But, it seems that as well as this misfortune both he and the servant were suffering from some kind of fever at the time. Fortunately, both recovered from their illnesses and Ralph Widdrington lived for some long time after "and was never molested".

In 1813, John Dobson carried out numerous alterations to the house for Ralph Riddell: the front door was moved from the south to the west side; he altered the windows and added the tower over the front door. The west front (featured) is now two-storeyed with tripartite windows. The tall, castellated centre bay has a castellated porch.

199

(Top):-
The private Roman Catholic chapel, which was added to the main house in 1813 by John Dobson has a three-light mullioned and transomed window with arched lights.

(Bottom, left):-
The chapel (right) and the north face of the Grange.

At the same time as he remodelled the house John Dobson also laid out the grounds "in a characteristically early 19th century Picturesque manner".

The garden (south) side (above, left) is two-storeyed: it has five, recessed, tripartite windows. This front was remodelled by John Dobson "from the existing 17th century house".

The alterations and additions to the east side of the house have clearly upset the symmetry of the façade. The two tripartite windows on the extreme left seem somewhat incongruous and the alteration from three-storey to two-storey has likewise destroyed the balance of the east front (below).

The Hall has a hipped ro[
two storeys and five ba[
The main entrance on [
south front is by a Tusc[
porch.

John Dobson is believed [
have carried out alterations [
the house, between 1828 a[
1830, for John Smart.

The east front of the Hall ha[
tall, central window w[
intersecting-style tracery.

Not far from Tynemouth Priory and Castle and on the top of John Dobson's monument, situated at the mouth of the River Tyne, is John Graham Lough's twenty-three feet tall statue of Admiral Cuthbert Collingwood. The admiral gazes out to sea. Below, on the plinth, are four of the cannon from Collingwood's ship, the Royal Sovereign.

The inscription on the monument reads:-

'This monument was erected n 1845, by public subscription, to the memory of Admiral Lord Collingwood who, in the Royal Sovereign, on the 21st of October 1805, led the British fleet into action at Trafalgar and sustained the sea fight for upwards of an hour before the other ships were within gunshot, which caused Nelson to exclaim: "See how that noble fellow Collingwood takes his ships into action".'

The Percy Chapel   (Tynemouth Priory)

'The chapel has a vaulted roof with curiously intersecting ribs terminating in three bosses ('studs' or 'raised ornaments') adorned with figures of the Saviour, the Virgin Mary and the Twelve Apostles, surrounded by legends now near effaced.

Several heraldic bearings of the Percy family are sculptured in this chapel and the arms of the Delaval family can still be seen on the inside of the door.'

Light gets into the tiny chapel (which only measures some eighteen feet by twelve) through the 'wheel' window in the east wall and the broad windows in the north and south walls.

This little chapel, was, for some time, used by the Board of Ordnance as a powder magazine but when its historical importance (it dates from the 15th century) was finally recognised it was carefully restored by John Dobson in 1852.

The castle is believed to have been built by one of the Umfraville family. In 1348 the manor passed, by marriage, into the Heron family, to whom it then belonged for some three centuries.

Legend had it that "when the heron should be seen charging through a fence instead of flying over it, the extinction of the family was near at hand". In fact, the last of the Herons to occupy the castle was Sir Harry, who sold both the castle and the estate around the end of the 17th century. The manor house was added to the Pele Tower, or Keep, in the reign of James I, by Cuthbert Heron whose initials and the date, 1621, are cut in stone above the south entrance.

Many fine houses were improved in the 18th century, by the replacement of sash windows. Between 1734 and 1754 the windows between the three arms of the 'E' shaped south front were sashed and 'Georgianised' by John Reed the elder. However, in 1819, John Reed the younger, having employed John Dobson to carry out some alterations to the house, instructed him to replace the sash windows, in the bows, with transomes and mullions.

The 'E'-shaped south front.

In times of great danger the cattle were sheltered for safety in a vaulted ground-floor room: above this was a guard-room and, on the third floor, above the guard-room, were the quarters where the family took sanctuary. The Manor House is crenellated; the 14th century Tower is not but it does have three tiers of what Pevsner calls "dummy Georgian windows" to balance the façade. The Tower's "crowning-motif" consists of four, circular, corbelled-out bartizans or corner turrets.

A church has stood on this site for more than twelve hundred years. The Saxon church of King Ceolwulf of Northumbria was given to the Abbot and monks of Holy Island, in 737.

It is highly unlikely that this first church survived the devastating raids of the Danes in the following century.

Remains of the next (stone built) Saxon church have been discovered beneath the present chancel arch, where a small cross marks the place where the altar stood.

This early church as the scene of a terrible massacre, on Saturday, July 13th, 1174, when Duncan, the Earl of Fife – one of William the Lion's commanders – mercilessly slaughtered at least a hundred (some have put the figures as high as three hundred) men, women and children who had taken refuge in the church and nearby vicarage.

The present church of St Lawrence is "a very fine, large, post-Conquest, Romanesque building" and "unique in Northumberland in being a fairly complete Norman church". The tower (built c.1200) has a 14th century upper stage and has one of only two medieval spires to be found in the county (- the other is on St Bartholomew's Church in Newbiggin-by-the-Sea).   The 15th century porch has an upper room, called the Parvise, which was formerly a school-room: it was reached by a circular staircase. By the mid-19th century the church was in a ruinous state.

In 1860-61, John Dobson restored both the nave and the chancel.

The bridge, designed by John Dobson crosses the River Eden on the A69 trunk road from Hexham to Carlisle and divides the villages of Warwick Bridge, on the east side, from Warwick on the west.

Brick built, it has three fine, wide, segmental arches.

Pevsner and Faulkner and Greg all cite 1837 as the year of its construction yet the date stone clearly shows it was built, by William Denton, between 1833-35.

Peter Dixon Junior commissioned John Dobson to design his palatial mansion and the house was built between 1833 and 1837. Dixon was one of three brothers whose wealth came from the cotton industry. However, their good fortune lasted barely thirty years: the after-effects of the American Civil War led to the collapse of both their business and the health of Peter Dixon. He died in 1866; his two brothers had pre-deceased him in 1857 and 1860. In 1873 the estate, of house and surrounding fifty-one acres, was auctioned off and bought by a Cumbrian family trust. But after only a short time this too collapsed and Holme Eden was again put on the market. Learning that the building was in imminent danger of demolition and even though he had no particular use for it the house and estate were bought by a local landowner.

Thereafter, it remained empty and unused for the next eight years. The only interest shown in the property during that period came from a Carlisle company seriously wanting to convert Holme Eden into a sausage factory! Eventually, the owner bequeathed the house to a Benedictine Order and for the next sixty years Holme Eden was convent, home to some sixty nuns. This was when it became known as Holme Eden Abbey. In 1983, the Mother Superior died and as there were now only eight nuns in residence they were transferred elsewhere and the Church Authorities once again offered the house for sale.

It was bought by Mrs Doreen Parsons, who began an immediate programme of careful restoration. All the original keynote features of John Dobson's grand design were lovingly restored – the staircase, panelled doors, window shutters, stone fireplaces and ceilings… and much more. Holme Eden Abbey then became a Residential Retirement Home and it remained so until 1996 when Mrs Parsons retired. The house has, since its subsequent sale, been converted into luxury apartments, by Cumbrian Homes of Penrith, and is now called Holme Eden Hall.

Holme Eden Abbey is one of only two 'calendar houses' in the United Kingdom. It has three hundred and sixty-five windows, fifty-two chimneys, twelve corridors, four floors and seven exits. It is a grade listed building. In its appearance it reminds one very much of Beaufront Castle, near Hexham; a country house of 1836-41, for William Cuthbert and also by John Dobson.

Holme Eden Abbey is raised on a terrace, overlooking the River Eden.

Holme Eden Abbey is a "spectacular essay in red sandstone, notable for its Tudor elevations, towers, turrets and crenellations, as well as an interior that celebrates the plasterer's and gilders art'. Constructed in the Tudor style, this sumptuous mansion bristles with ornamental chimneys, high mullioned windows, a crenellated porch and cantilevered balcony. Many of the reception rooms have vaulted or coffered ceilings, some finely decorated and gilded, and there are dressed stone fireplaces with beautiful ceramic tile inserts.

All the interior stone and woodwork is of the very finest quality.

Shortly after moving into Holme Eden, Peter Dixon, a devout Christian, offered to build and endow a church for the district. It was recognised that a new church was needed as the existing Parish Church (at Wetheral) could "…. Not afford accommodation for more than one third of the inhabitants"; so Dixon's offer was gladly accepted by the Diocese of Carlisle.

Peter Dixon provided the land for a church; churchyard and burial ground met the cost of the building itself (said to have been about £1,500) and gave £2,500 (at 4% per annum) towards the stipend of the Vicar. The new church, dedicated in the name of St Paul, together with the surrounding churchyard, was consecrated by Hugh Percy, Bishop of Carlisle, on Tuesday, September 2nd, 1845.

The church was designed by John Dobson, and so, almost certainly was the adjacent vicarage.

Dobson's early training as a gardener gave him a special interest in the actual site of his buildings. It has been suggested he almost preferred the landscape surrounding his works to the buildings themselves, so it is easy to imagine that the beautiful site beside the River Eden that was put to his disposal for Holme Eden Church would give him special pleasure. The exterior of the building is virtually unchanged from Dobson's original building. It is a very simple design in red sandstone with a slate roof and consists of a nave, a small chancel with an apse at the east end, a spire, one hundred and ten feet tall at the west end over the entrance porch and a small vestry at the south-east corner.

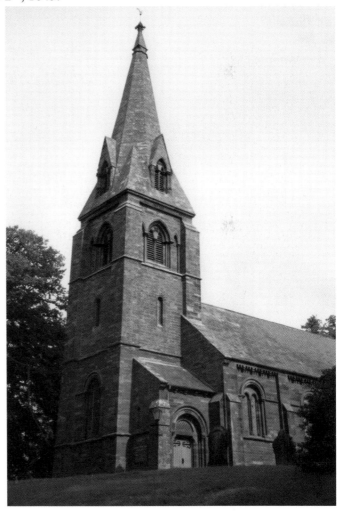

The Newcastle Courant of July 31st, 1830, tells us that in that year John Dobson added a gallery to the Church of St Nicholas. The church appears to be entirely of the 13th century and spires of the period are quite a rarity.

Some of the aisle windows are 19th century, as are those in the chancel.

The south porch, however, belongs entirely to the 13th century.

212

A monastery once stood on the site of the south garden. This was 'dissolved' a the time of the Reformation. The site was then occupied, in the 17th century, by a domestic farmhouse.

In the 18th century it became a dower-house for Shawdon Hall.

At the beginning of the 19th century John Dobson added the plain, classical south front.

The two-storey, five-bay south front has a central, open-pedimented doorway, sash windows and hipped roof.

The east front of Bolton Hall.

Thirston House(West Thirston, Felton, Morpeth)

The Statutory List of Buildings of Special Architectural Interest tells us that c.1820, John Dobson designed this fine house for the Newton family.

The two-storey, four-bay house is of dressed stone and has a hipped roof. The south front has a fine Tuscan porch and stepped entrance.

The west elevation also has four bays.

(right):-

The four column Tuscan porch.

The east side of the house is of particular interest.

It is likely that, like the west front the east side also had four bays and that the house had been extended northward and that the central, three-bay porch has been added at some later time.

The stonework to the right is entirely different and no effort has been made to match the window pattern of the original house. From an aesthetic point of view the appearance of the east side is so irregular as to spoil what could so easily have bee a sensible and sensitive addition to what is, after all, a fine 19th century dwelling.

The house was entirely remodelled inside, in 1912.

Holeyn Hall   (Wylam)

The Hall was built between 1850-53 for Edward James, a Tyneside lead merchant: the name of the original architect is unknown but we do know that in 1858 John Dobson added the tower (left) and the balustraded south front.

The James family moved to Swarland Hall, in 1876, and the estate was then purchased by Lt. Col. M C Woods, a Newcastle banker.

John Dobson was commissioned in 1858, to make "large additions" to the house, for Edward James.

Holeyn Hall was, for a time (- he bought the house in 1894) the home of Sir Charles Algernon Parsons. Parsons, an Irishman by birth, became an adopted son of the north-east. He invented and developed the steam-turbine and used it for marine propulsion in his famous "Turbinia" – now to be seen in the Discovery Museum, in Blandford Square, Newcastle.

Bradley Hall   (near Wylam)

The house was built in 1750, by James Paine, a London architect, for John Simpson, a Newcastle merchant – though an earlier property had occupied the site.

Bradley is a modest little house, claims Neville Whittaker, with some curious idiosyncrasies in the façade design. The cornice in the centre pedimented section is truncated to appear only over the side bays … and the main string course changes level abruptly from side to centre bays. The central first floor window has the pronounced 'ear pieces' which were to become so much a feature of Paine's designs.

217

The south front (above) has seven bays; the three central bays are under an open pediment and three of the windows in the central, projecting section are pedimented. The doorway has a Tuscan surround. Inside, two rooms have fine, rococo stucco ceilings and there is a staircase with a delightful Chippendale fretwork balustrade which, Mrs Simpson assures me, is the only one of its kind in the entire country.

Around the year 1813, John Dobson moved the main entrance from the south to the east side, for the first Lord Ravensworth. It opens into a corridor behind the three large south rooms.

Part Two

The City

of

Newcastle upon Tyne.

P M Horsley, in his book Eighteenth Century Newcastle, tells us something of the early Barber-Surgeons' Hall.

The Barber-Surgeons had no permanent headquarters until 1648, when the Corporation gave them a site at the Manors (at an annual rent of six shillings and eightpence), together with stone for a building and the provision of a medical herb garden. The stone came from the dismantling of the Priory of the Austin Friars.

Celia Fiennes, an intrepid traveller during the reign of William and Mary, noted in her diary that she had been far more impressed by the equipment inside the building rather than the building itself.

She describes 'with undisguised relish' the convenience of the dissecting table, with chairs for the spectators; the skeletons – 'one had had the flesh boyled off and so some of ye ligeament remained and dryed with it, and so the parts were held together by its own muscles and sinews" – and a stuffed human skin, which she had not been averse to handling. Horsley tells us that in 1711 the price of a human skeleton in good condition was £6-6-0; by 1891 this had risen to ten pounds: that of a gorilla cost thirty-five pounds!

In 1851 the School of Medicine and Surgery moved into the new building (designed by John Dobson) on Victoria Street.

"This is a major essay in Dobson's now favoured Italian Renaissance style – later marred by ugly brick extensions." (Faulkner and Greg).

The new Hall was paid for by the York, Newcastle and Berwick Railway Company whose recent expansion to the Manors had necessitated the demolition of the early 18th century Hall.

I am indebted to the two above writers for the following information on the 'new' Barber-Surgeons' Hall:

"It is a detached, rectangular building of two storeys. On the first floor were lecture and dissecting rooms and a large museum, illuminated partly from above. Its principal, or south, façade is a symmetrical composition with five bays (the outer two projecting with rusticated quoins) completed by a large cornice, dwarf attic and (originally) tall, rusticated chimneys.

The upper windows of the central section form a Renaissance-style arcade with keystones decorated with the 'Aesculapian' snakes, while

The Hall has been described as "one of (Dobson's) most dignified and successful later works".

221

Mackenzie describes the lantern tower as "one of the noblest and most admired structures that adorn our island".

Lyall Wilkes tells us that "when the lantern tower... which Robert Stephenson calculated weighed seventy tons, was in danger of collapse, John Dobson, in circumstances of difficulty and some danger, succeeded in widening the foundations of the 194 feet tower, supporting the walls by buttresses, taking down and restoring the pinnacles and all parts of the superstructure destroyed by age, and was particularly proud of the fact that nothing was to be seen, externally, of this restoration". The Newcastle Daily Chronicle (Monday, January 9th, 1865) tells us a little more:-

"The tower of St Nicholas Church, which is the pride of Newcastle, was in imminent danger of falling, through the cutting away (by the cupidity of those having a vested interest in the internment fee) of the piers which supported the whole structure. Mr Dobson took in hand to stay the ruin and actually underset the foundation of a tower, 194 feet high, supported the walls by buttresses, which he metamorphosed into a convenient Gothic porch and took down and restored the pinnacles and other parts of the superstructure decayed by age, and of all this work, executed under circumstances of great difficulty, no trace but the porticos and the buttresses can be detected by an ordinary observer."

The best (and fullest) account, however, is to be found in Archaelogia Aeliana, by H L Honeyman. He writes:-

"In 1827 one of the pinnacles of the steeple was observed by 'totter' when the bells were rung. On examination it was found that the lead coverings having been stripped by the wind, the iron cramps inserted in 1795 had rusted and fractured the stonework, while the cement fillings had perished. New copper cramps were inserted and Roman cement fillings were required... small pinnacles renewed in mason work, vanes required and regilt. " The work of repair to the steeple went on slowly while the Corporation and churchwardens argued about liability.

The scaffolding erected in 1827 was still standing in 1829 (and in that year the wardens had a case stated for the opinion of J Chitty of 6, Chantry Lane). Therein they mention that 'the Belfry windows are now so much out of repair that it is dangerous to ring the Bells lest the stone Mullions of the Windows, which are in a very decayed and rotten state, should fall down...'

Incidentally, in 1831 Major George Anderson, a generous benefactor of Newcastle churches, left £500 for a new bell. He had reason to think kindly of the bells of St Nicholas for they rang merrily to celebrate his return from gaol, where he had been incarcerated for pulling the nose of the Town Clerk, John Clayton!

The Tower continued to crack and tilt southwards until it was fully ten inches off the perpendicular.

In 1832 reports were obtained from John Dobson and also from John Green. Dobson proposed to underpin the tower itself, at an estimated cost of £1,200, insert binding courses of cube stones, from pillar to pillar, and introduce iron tie-rods at several different points in the superstructure, particularly in the tower and south arcade of the nave: the west-most arch seems to have been restored at this time.

Green proposed to erect new western transepts as buttresses to the tower and make them the starting points for a compete re-facing of the church, in the Perpendicular style of Gothic architecture.

Ultimately it was agreed that Dobson should be the Corporation's architect and preserve the tower at the joint expense of church and town, and that, to satisfy the clamour for visible buttresses Green's scheme should then proceed at the church's cost.

The Cathedral's magnificent lantern tower.

During Dobson's underpinning several stone coffins were found just under the pavement on the west side of the tower, proving that the churchyard had formerly extended over what is now St Nicholas' Street.

In 1833, the church-wardens (being £1000 in debt for their share of the work on the tower)... called a public meeting and appealed for funds. There was a quick and generous response... so that in 1834, the work which had commenced on the south side was continued on the north and finally, in 1836, the west window was rebuilt and the tower entrance doorway reconstructed." "Most of Green's work" adds Honeyman, "was bolder and coarser in detail than Dobson's and their share (John Green and his son, Benjamin) of St Nicholas is no exception". Honeyman then goes on to give a list of the repairs modifications and 'improvements' carried out by the Greens concluding, rather sarcastically that "doubtless in time they would have rebuilt the whole church but death removed John Green in 1852 and his son in 1858."

In 1863 the author of the Daily Journal's Guide to Newcastle wrote that the tower needed repair, "it being hazardous to ring a full peal owing to the dilapidated state of the belfry mason work".

John Dobson had prepared a specification for its restoration, the present condition of the steeple being quite dangerous.

"It is not uncommon", said one observer, "in boisterous weather to see a group of people anxiously watching the steeple, which they declare may be seen swaying to and fro with the wind."

But Dobson died in January 1865 and when, in 1867, the north side of the tower (lacking the buttresses promised in 1832) began to subside, it was Sir George Gilbert School RA who underpinned it and rebuilt the crown and lantern, restored them to the vertical so that they are no longer quite in the same line as the tower.

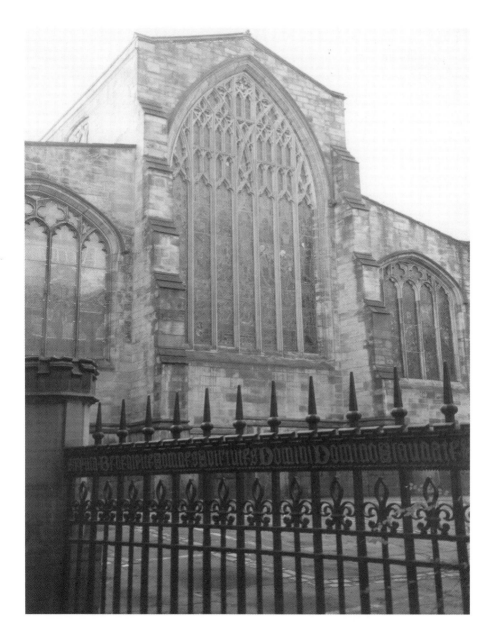

"The deaths of the Greens", writes Honeyman, "left the way open for the return of John Dobson, now in his seventies but still an incorrigible 'improver'.

He rebuilt the east gable in 1859, with a single enormous window instead of the two it originally held". "This did not meet with the entire approval of our Society," remarks Honeyman, "and at the September meeting Dobson gave a not very convincing apologia for his scheme."

Apparently 'the stonework was not in good condition'. The church authorities wished the new gable to be 'Decorated' and the architect took credit for having instead, adhered to the 'Perpendicular' style of the original, if not to its form.

The original Church of St Nicholas was founded by St Osmond, Bishop of Salisbury, in the time of William the Conqueror. Henry I granted it to the canons of St Mary's, Carlisle: this building was destroyed by fire in 1216.

The present church (it became a Cathedral in 1882 when Newcastle became a city) dates back to the middle of the 14th century: the crown spire was added in 1470.

"Its arches and knotted pinnacles, in every direction, are thrown into lines of great delicacy; and at four points of view the light through its centre assumes the form of a well-proportioned wheat sheaf."

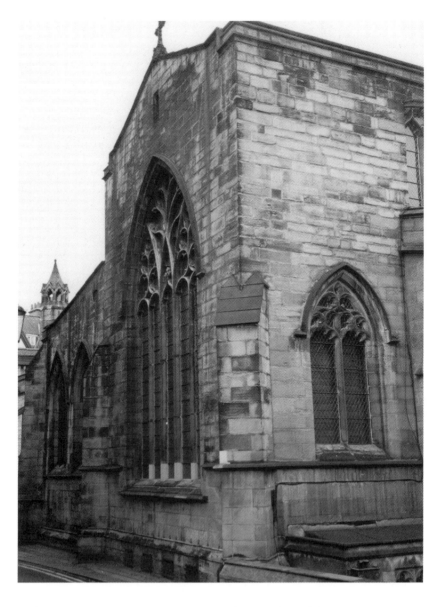

In 1824 John Dobson painstakingly restored the remains of the north transept window.

Newcastle's Railway Station is a fine tribute to the architect's imagination but, in truth, it is a pale shadow of what John Dobson originally intended. Had his plan been adopted, exactly as he designed it it would, in all likelihood, have been the magnificent climax of Dobson's successful life's work: it was not to be.

The thirty-six pairs of Roman Doric columns; the parallel port-cochères; the great central portico with its giant, seated figures – all of these (and more) were features of Dobson's original 'grand scheme'.

Unfortunately (and this was by no means the only time his ideas were thwarted by a lack of money), the crash in the railway stock market compelled Dobson to compromise his designs within the constraints of the finances available to him.

But, as W W Tomlinson was later to write: "...Even without the arcades and portico (the portico was added in 1863, by Thomas Prosser), the stately line of building facing Neville Street, 593½ feet in length with its simple and apposite Doric ornament could not fail to produce a striking effect. Fortunately, no alteration of plan was required for the interior of the station; the bold, curving lines of which, in building, roof and platform, and the long succession of receding arches carved in finely moulded imposts over doors and windows from end to end, give so agreeable an impression of unity and simplicity of design."

This imposing structure took the place of a small building, which was the terminus of the Shields and also the Berwick Railway. It cost £120,000 and covers about eleven acres.

The architect's daughter tells us that her father spent three days in a railway station watching the issue of tickets, the passengers getting in and out of the trains, the departure and arrival of trains, in order that he might obtain a thorough knowledge of the sort of work to be performed there, and so harmonize the character of the architecture with the purpose of the building. The result of this careful study is evident in the arrangement of the platforms and the various offices attached.

Dobson's original plans were altered as regards the exterior of the building when the walls were half up as the company (the York, Newcastle and Berwick Railway Company) decided to bring the chief offices from York to Newcastle. Consequently, Dobson was compelled to rearrange the entire design, making the building two storeys instead of one and abandoning the noble classic colonnade which was to have stretched the whole length of the building, with a portico in the centre double the width of the colonnade.

However, Honeyman writes that, "…. The Central Station which, had it been completed as first designed by Dobson would, even now, have ranked among the world's finest railway stations – even as it is, few stations, other than termini, excel it".

The iron-worked roofing was unique at the time. Dobson devised a process which pressed the iron out between rollers instead of cutting it from flattened plates (the work was provided by Hawk, Crawley & Co. of Gateshead) and Dobson's invention, now universally copied, won him a prize at the Paris Exposition.

G M Saxby, station-master in 1911, had this to say of the building – "Architecturally, the station as originally designed, had no compeer among English stations. The architect has given us Vanburgh's best qualities without his alloy, his vigour without his coarseness, his boldness in massing and outlines without his rude capriciousness."
Elsewhere it has been said, "Inside, it is all space and light, full of elegant curves. The railway lines curve, the platforms curve, and the high vaulted cast-iron and glass roof curves too."

The Central Station was opened by Queen Victoria and Prince Albert on August 29th, 1850. The day was declared a public holiday and local manufacturers were asked to put their fires out between eleven o'clock in the morning and two in the afternoon, so as not to cloud the momentous occasion. Local legend has it that this was Victoria's last visit to Newcastle. After the celebration banquet, the manager of the hotel had the temerity to present Her Majesty with the bill!

She was not amused and, thereafter, whenever she passed through the town on her journey north to Balmoral she ordered all the window blinds to be closed until her train was clear of Newcastle.

Dr S M Linsley writes: "Newcastle Central Station, with its classical frontage and innovative train-shed roof, was the physical embodiment of John Dobson's philosophy".

A less than glamorous view of the station with the tracks leading away east. It does however serve to give an impression of the actual size of the station – it covers some eleven acres and was constructed between 1847-50.

Grey, writing his Survey of Newcastle, in 1649, claimed that St Andrew's is the oldest of the four 'city' churches.

Others have also said that the style of the building shows this to be the case, 'and so tradition has always held it to be so'. The general opinion seems to be that the present building was begun somewhere between 1150-1175, though a small Saxon church may have existed on the site.

(left) "The sturdy west tower… with its large, south-west clasping buttress, was surmounted by a gun in the Civil War of the 1640s."

(below) The south transept was remodelled, in neo-Norman style, by John Dobson in 1844.

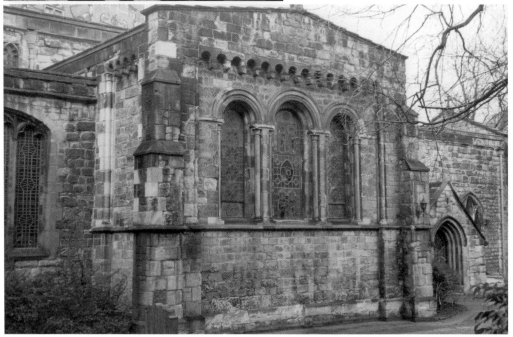

A Church of St John the Baptist has stood on this site for more than eight hundred years. Not many early fragments still remain visible but these are enough to show that a small Norman church , consisting of only nave and chancel, stood here at least as early as the first half of the twelfth century (1100-1150).

The most obvious relic from this early Norman church is the round-headed arch in the north wall of the chancel. That is probably the oldest wall in the building and may include stones taken from the nearby Roman Wall. Basically a church of the 14th and 15th centuries though its date of consecration is somewhere between 1145 and 1245; it has been described as "an oasis among modern buildings".

Grey called it "a pretty little church…. because it much resembles a cross".

The west tower is believed to be fifteenth century and has "quite elaborate pinnacles".

Various dates have been attributed to John Dobson relating to work he carried out on St John's Church.

One report suggests he restored the chancel (now the Lady Chapel), and which contains a window including fragments of medieval glass with the earliest known representation of the arms of Newcastle, in 1829 and refitted it in 1859.

Another alleges he restored the church's chancel and gables, in 1829. Dobson's daughter, Margaret Jane, asserts her father designed the altar railings and reredos, in 1859.

Geoffrey Purves claims that Dobson rebuilt the south and east walls of the chancel in 1848.

This latter date is probably the more accurate and is supported by a report in the Newcastle Courant of July 2nd, 1848.

The Church of St Thomas the Martyr   (Newcastle upon Tyne)

In 1820 a decision was made to demolish the Chapel of the Bridge of Tyne, situated at the north end of the old Tyne Bridge, Sandhill (in 1770 the west end had already been demolished and in 1782 it had been further reduced in size).

At their own expense the Corporation of Newcastle decided to erect a new chapel at Barras Bridge, on Magdalene Meadow, which belonged to St Mary Magdalene Hospital.

The Act of Parliament for the erection of the new chapel was given the Royal Assent on June 21st, 1827. In July 1827, plans by John Dobson were approved by the Corporation to erect a new chapel. This would cost some £4,500 and would seat some twelve hundred people.

Designed by John Dobson and built between 1827 and 1830, it was consecrated on October 19th, 1830. Described by Edinburgh architect to John Clayton, the Town Clerk, as "one of the most chase buildings … anywhere in the Kingdom"; another critic has remarked, "the slenderness of the structure is remarkable: the balcony was an unfortunate addition".

John Dobson's Covered Fish Market of 1823-6 replaced the ancient but now decayed Maison Dieu, originally a charity almshouse but by then used only as a quayside warehouse.

Dobson's addition to the Guildhall (of the Fish Market and new premises above for the Merchant Adventurer's Guild) is an example of small scale, urban Greek Revival. A semi-circular colonnade (later but sensitively filled in) of unfluted Doric columns supports two storeys of plain windows. It is linked to the older building by one bay, an archway and two… tripartite windows.

Despite some initial hostility from the fishwives for their new market the building was considered "one of the handsomest ornaments of the town having cleared the Sandhill of the number of fish stalls and widened the entrance to the Quay".

In her Memoir, Margaret Jane Dobson tells the following charming story: "The good ladies who presided over the stalls seriously objected to being removed from their old quarters and for some time Mr Dobson received such an impolite reception from them that he was obliged to avoid their presence. But when bad weather came and they realised the comfort of their new abode they relented and a deputation of fair dames arrived at his residence in New Bridge Street with a peace offering of fish for a Christmas dinner. Ever after that he was their 'cannie Mr Dobson'".

In 1948, poet, broadcaster and writer on architecture, John Betjeman, visited Newcastle to give a lecture at the Literary and Philosophical Society. Known to much prefer the countryside to urban life and impassioned in his abhorrence of modern architecture he was clearly overwhelmed by the vision of Grey Street and his reaction is worth repeating here:

"As for the curve of Grey Street, I shall never forget seeing it to perfection; trafficless, on a misty Sunday morning. Not even Regent Street, old Regent Street, London, can compare with that subtle curve."

The west side of the street, looking north, and the magnificent 'curve' referred to by John Betjeman.

There has always been controversy over who should receive the greatest credit for the design of "the finest street in our city, with its magnificent curve, built to a master plan…." Too many plans, drawings and records have been lost over the years (if, indeed, they ever existed) to guarantee any degree of certainty but current opinion suggest that John Dobson was responsible for the east side of the street, between Shakespeare Street and Mosley Street, while the "beautiful and elaborately designed west side" was the work of John Wardle, one of Richard Grainger's esteemed architects. The Northumberland Directory for 1854, has this to say: "Grey Street is the great work. The front and entire decoration of the houses are of solid stone; the stone is of a warm, rich colour – the ranges excel those of Edinburgh, in being more ornate, and they excel those of Regent Street, in London, as truly as good stone excels shabby stucco."

The Directory goes on to give a comprehensive account of the buildings and a detailed description of their architecture, on both sides of the street, but it would be perhaps inappropriate or at least unnecessary to reproduce this here since it would probably be of greatest interest only to those readers who have a professional interest in architecture or, as lay-men, a more than passing interest in such matters. For those who would like to learn more from "the best short description ever written about this street "reference to the Directory would appear essential. Failing this, let me recommend a copy of Tyneside Classical by Wilkes and Dodds, with particular reference to chapter four – "The Crowning Achievement".

A further short extract from the Directory might, however, be considered both apposite and helpful: "At the east side of Grey Street, we find the entire length distributed into five architectural compartments, separated by the crossing of other streets."

(*Author's note: we need not concern ourselves with four of these since they do not relate directly to Dobson but are explained on page 90 of Tyneside Classical).

"The first, or southern compartment, from Mosley Street to Shakespeare Street, has in the centre a colonnade of lofty Corinthian columns with wings, having pilasters and balustrades…"

A fuller description of Dobson's architecture on this side of the street is given by Collard and Ross, in their Architectural and Picturesque Views of Newcastle upon Tyne (1847). This reads: "The second storey of the centre (of the east side of Grey Street) consists of a recessed range of lofty fluted columns of a Corinthian order, and the upper storey of which is adorned with a row of square vases. On each side of this centre is a house with projecting wings, the upper storeys supported by square pilasters, above which are elegant mouldings and the attics of the wings are surmounted by neat balustrades. A large window in the second storey of each wing is ornamented with a neat pediment in Italian style and a balustrade runs along the centre of the second storey, from wing to wing. Ranges of buildings sweep off to the north and south of the houses just noticed, terminated by projecting wings decorated in a nearly similar manner to the houses immediately flanking the centre. A similar style prevails on this side of the street after passing High Bridge to the corner of Shakespeare Street."

A design of typical simplicity – short window pilasters and giant, framing pilasters, the latter with Corinthian capitals.

This block has retained its balustrades: other buildings further down the street have not.

John Dobson's architecture on the east side of Grey Street is generally simpler and more subdued and perhaps less dramatic than John Wardle's west side. Sadly, however, much of Dobson's original work – from Norfolk House (Shakespeare Street) right down to Mosley Street – has, since 1836, been either, repaired, restored, rebuilt or remodelled. Numbers 52-78 (above) include a small corner pavilion and a large, seven-window-wide pavilion separated by a plain section that was originally four houses. 52-60 were repaired and extended (to the rear of the premises) in 1996. The Edwardian shop front, of number 52, and the balustrades above number 60 were also restored at that time.

This was Dobson's "grand centre piece" already referred to.

Two thirds of the original façade, however, were demolished and rebuilt in 1910 in – as David Lovie describes it – "a heavy and inappropriate classical style".

Fortunately, in a 1969 restoration scheme these alterations were removed and everything except the ground floor was replaced in the style of Dobson's original work of c.1836; faithfully reproducing his columns, cornices, upper floor windows and even the decorative urns.

Grand pavilion and plain, two-house section. The large pavilion, once described as "a house with projection wings", still retains its attic and first floor balustrade. The ground floor, using local natural stone 'columns', is a twentieth century alteration.

Here we have one of John Dobson's "grand pavilions", on the east side of Grey Street – though this is far more decorative than Dobson's other pavilions on the street.

It is considered somewhat out of character with Dobson's usual style and has led some commentators to suggest it may be the work of W L Newcombe who, in 1890, added an ornate Victorian ground floor and extended the interior.

Further alterations were made to the interior c.1980.

An 18th century building (with cellars) already occupied this corner site and it may be that rather than demolish it completely Grainger simply "tarted it up" – refurbishing the interior while Dobson used an elaborate Italian design to remodel the upper building.

This was the last piece of the "jigsaw" on Grey Street to be completed (on the junction of Mosley Street) and it required a grant from the Corporation, in 1842, for it to be so.

For many years it stood as an eyesore at the bottom of Grey Street (unused and unloved) … its restoration was finally completed c.2003.

Eldon Square was designed by Thomas Oliver, planned by John Dobson and built by Richard Grainger, between 1825 and 1831.

In his book "New Picture of Newcastle" (published in 1831), by Thomas Oliver, the author says of Eldon Square –

"Mr T Oliver (architect) was requested to prepare a design, plans of which together with a model of the same, were submitted for inspection at a meeting of the Common Council when the opinion of Mr Dobson (architect) was taken, who afterwards furnished a plan containing several alterations …..

Eldon Square, with the exception of the centre building, is now complete: the three sides are of polished stone, to an elevation designed by Mr Dobson…"

This extract from Oliver's 1831 publication seems to suggest that Dobson's role in the construction of the Square was no more than that of 'advisory architect' on the main plan and design of the main facades – the main glory of Eldon Square.

The three great blocks of the Square, the east and west of twenty-seven bays and the north of thirty-nine, were each symmetrical, their angles accented with Doric pilasters. The first floor, with very tall windows had cast-iron balconies with Greek honeysuckle décor.

Eldon Square was unprecedented in Newcastle for its size, uniformity and building quality. Most of Newcastle's houses at this time were still built of brick: the houses in Eldon Square were faced with fine, ashlar masonry – one of the earliest uses of stone for domestic houses in Newcastle.

On the centre block there was intended to be a six-column portico – but this never materialised.

Between the ground and first floors there were cast-iron balconies with a Greek, honeysuckle decoration.

247

Archaelogia Aeliana (vol. XXIX) says that Eldon Square was Dobson's first known attempt at designs of town terraces, his previous practice having been entirely in the alteration and enlargement of country houses and the design of Presbyterian and Methodist chapels. It is one of his best and we cannot now regret his poaching on what might have been (Thomas) Oliver's preserve.

Truly, these were fashionable terraces, described by one writer as – "the finest town houses built in the north"; and by another as the genteelest and best built part of the town".

The spaciousness of the Square was a thing quite unheard of in Newcastle and this at a time when the town's buildings were still principally of brick and with most of its streets dirty, narrow and irregular. With regard to the proposed portico on the centre block, Eaneas Mackenzie hints that there may have been a difference of opinion over the design or that, perhaps, Dobson (not for the first or last time) met with some form of 'obstruction'. Whatever the reason, the portico never materialised.

Alas; only the east side of the Square remains today (2008). The wretched shopping centre that now bears its name was built, by Philistines masquerading as planners and developers, between 1969-75, and was the cause of the destruction of the north and west sides of a Square containing the most fashionable houses in Newcastle.

Two thirds of the Square were demolished to make way for the Eldon Square Shopping Centre … an act of unspeakable vandalism.
Featured presently, in the grass centre of what still remains, stands the War memorial of c.1920, by Charles Hardman, topped by a bronze statue of St George.

Newe House, or Anderson Place as it was renamed by its builder-owner, was a mansion started in 1580, in the style of a country seat laid out in a large, formal garden, right in the middle of a crowded walled town. By the 1930s, and despite its apparent grandeur, it had obviously become an anachronism and if Richard Grainger's ambitious plans for the development of the town centre were to be realised, then it had to go. He eventually secured its purchase for £50,000. The site was to be the heart of his commercial and residential development; a network of streets and a covered market, designed by John Dobson.

In 1834 the Corporation, encouraged by John Clayton the Town Clerk, did indeed accept Grainger's plans and on the 24th October, 1835, at a cost of £36,290, within one year of the contract being signed, the Markets were officially opened.

They were the most successful attempt to attract a traffic-free shopping precinct Newcastle had ever achieved, not only because owing to the low rents and overheads they could (and still do) sell goods cheaper than shops in the main streets.

The Market is divided into two parts – the Vegetable Market and the Butchers' Market. The open-plan Vegetable Market, with a complex roof structure, designed originally without the cast-iron pillars inserted, apparently at the request of the Corporation's architects (the fine timbered roof has now, unfortunately, been covered by the Corporation) has an avenue which – according to 'experts' varies in length from 313 feet to 338 feet, but which they all agree is forty feet high.

It contained fifty-five shops when it opened.

The whole was contained within four streets of shops and houses "surpassing anything in street architecture hitherto witnessed in this neighbourhood". Many traders moved here from the Quayside, keen to take advantage of the new developments – at the same time accelerating the decline of the riverside.

Dobson's enormous covered market, protected by a massive glass roof, the largest in the country, was of great architectural elegance. It covers several acres and the interior consists of five longitudinal avenues and four transverse ones, each twelve feet wide, and presents a succession of arched passages between the larger avenues.

The Butchers' Market was housed in a network of four avenues, each 338 feet long with pilastered arcades with classical detailing – 360 windows, fanlights and wood cornices. All told, the market contained one hundred and eighty-eight shops. David Bean's colourful account of the Market's official opening tells us that "the Corporation organised a grand public dinner inside and two thousand people turned up to admire 'the most magnificent markets in the world' and the bazaar of shops within which struck the stranger with astonishment and wonder, beyond description".

There were, in fact, two public dinners, both in the Vegetable Market. Ladies were placed up in the gallery while fountains (copied from Rome's Borghese Palace) played below.

"The effect," wrote one reporter, "was indescribably grand. The partial exclusion of daylight and the substitution of gas-lamps gave the magnificent scene a dioramic effect."

By the beginning of the 20th century the appearance of the Butchers' market had changed dramatically. Jack Common gives this colourful description, in his book Kidder's Luck –

"A vast covered enclosure in which many sawdust-sprinkled aisles ran between the stalls, not only of the butchers and book-sellers, drapers, ironmongers, cheap jewellers … glittering quicksands of proletarian penny-swallowing.

The aisles echoed to the yells and yodels of salesmen, everyone of them selling cheaper than the man next door."

"The Butcher and Green Market (ie the present Grainger Market), with the block of houses enclosing them, were designed by the late Mr John Dobson ..." – a statement expressed in the Newcastle Daily Chronicle of March 21st, 1868, and which has never seriously been contradicted.

The east front of the Market (featured) has giant fluted Corinthian pilasters on both the wings and the central pavilion. Such was the popularity of Grainger Street in the late 19th and 20th centuries that it became the main commercial street of the City. This inevitably led to a number of alterations, expansions and modifications to the properties: roofs were raised or flattened on several premises; shop fronts have been altered several times; canopies were added but, thankfully, later removed.

The west front of the market follows the same pattern as the east on Grainger Street, except here the eight bays on the central pavilion are plain and the fluted pilasters are conspicuously absent.

The north front of the Market follows Dobson's usual pattern of wings, plain links and pavilions.

Grainger Street and Clayton Street, being the town's principal streets, their architecture is more elaborate, more decorative.

On Nelson Street only the wings have decorative pilasters, the rest is fairly plain.

The Market's south front on Nun Street, is identical to that on Nelson Street: the giant pilasters are again confined to the east wings.

A short terrace of houses, of the early 1830s, on the east side of the Great North Road, has been attributed to John Dobson.

Number 14 has three short, individual balconies. There is a single balcony from 16-18 (inc.): number 20 has no balcony.

The surviving balconies, with Greek honeysuckle motif, are similar (but not identical) to those in Eldon Square.

They appear to be decorative rather than functional though whether this has always been so I cannot say.

The houses are four storeyed (including basements). There are two projecting wings, each three bays wide: the remainder of the terrace is slightly recessed and is nine bays wide.

Described as a "substantial, three-storeyed three-bay house with a dainty honeysuckle frieze and Ionic portico".

The house, built in 1823 to the architect's own designs, was originally of ashlar and though it has been painted over several times since then "it still displays the crisp simplicity of Dobson's 1820s classicism". The original façade was uncomplicated by an entrance, which was placed to the side. There was a long garden at the rear of the house where Dobson kept his collection of architectural fragments.

After having suffered a severe stroke in 1862, at the age of seventy-four, John Dobson died here, in New Bridge Street, on January 8th, 1865. His house was later bought by one Henry Donnelly and converted into a lodging house.

Since then it has endured the indignity of becoming a dance hall (the Oxford Galleries) and is now a nightclub, Ikon.

The (Castle) Keep   (Newcastle upon Tyne)

Nothing now remains of the earth –and-timber fortress built c.1080 by Robert Curthose, the son of William the Conqueror, on the site of some ancient fort, which caused it to be called the 'New Castle'.

The New Castle, as it remains now, consists only of the great Norman Keep, built by Henry II, between 1127-77, at a cost of £911-10-9.

In 1644 the Keep saw its last fight when Sir John Marley, the mayor, who had taken refuge there, finally surrendered to the Scots. The Keep fell into decay and it remained neglected until Newcastle Corporation bought it for £600 in 1808.

Military occupation of the Keep came to an end in 1819 and the last of its prisoners was released from its dungeon in 1828.

In 1847 John Dobson carried out extensive restoration of the Keep, including all the battlements and paying special attention to the Chapel and the entrance to the Great Hall.

Accommodation in the Hall soon became inadequate however and so, in 1855, the Society of Antiquaries accepted Dobson's proposed plan to provide more space. Unfortunately the necessary funds for such an enterprise were never forthcoming and so the architect's plans were shelved.

The Keep measures approximately sixty-two feet by fifty-six feet. The ground floor is made up of the outer gateway, into the fore-building, with the beginning of the staircase, originally with a gate tower over and two vaulted rooms only accessible by a spiral stair from the second floor. The main room is an oblong with a circular, central pier, . Accessible from the spiral stair, by means of an inner chamber, is the Chapel, taking up space in the fore-building below the upper parts of the staircase. The platform dates from 1809 and, like the battlements, is by Dobson.

Newcastle's Keep is one of the best preserved in England, a typical specimen of Norman-Transitional architecture, although the barrel-vaulted roof of brick, the battlements, the flag turret and the wooden floor of the hall are all early 19th century additions. At one time cannon were fired from the roof, each day at noon, but the practice was soon discontinued because of damage caused to surrounding buildings.

In 1848, to celebrate the restoration of the Keep, the Society of Antiquaries held a banquet there. John Dobson's proposed plan of 1855 to organise more exhibition space, while accepted by the Society, was eventually shelved through lack of funds.

The Lying-in-Hospital was moved from Rosemary Lane, in 1826, to a new building, planned by John Dobson, at the junction of Croft Street and New Bridge Street.

In 1858 it was decided to amalgamate the outdoor charity for poor women, lying-in at their own homes, with the lying-in-hospital. Thereafter, the combined charities, under the title 'The Lying-in-Hospital and Outdoor Charity for Poor Married Women' continued to occupy the New Bridge Street building until it was taken over as a studio by the British Broadcasting Corporation.

Described as "a beautiful little building in pale ashlar", with perpendicular tracery in the oriel over the Tudor-arched doorway and cusped windows and canopies, it was Dobson's first important building in the Gothic style. Actually designed in 1825, it is said he made no charge for his plans for this "charitable asylum for poor, married, pregnant women".

While it was the property of the BBC for a number of years it is now the city headquarters for the Newcastle Building Society (since 1994). The hospital is now called Portland House.

The Market Keeper's House, Cattle Market
Collard and Ross 1841

This print of 1841 is included by kind permission of Tyne & Wear Development Corporation.

The House (or Cattle Market Office) was built in 1841, for a sum – according to the Newcastle Journal of January 29th, 1997 – of £900. It was designed by John Dobson who charged a fee of £40. The House (or Cottage) was once home to two families – that of the cattle market keeper and the toll collector. In 1910 Barclays took it over as a bank and other users have included the Tyneside Fat Trading Company and Homebilt Timber (as illustrated, right).

The House or cottage was empty from 1990 but the architect involved in its restoration, Allan Guthrie of Ainsworth Spark Associates, was reported in the Journal newspaper –saying that the house would be thoroughly repaired, the stonework cleaned, a new roof put in place and a clock installed in the tower.

He added that not only would the house be brought back into use but that it would become a focal point within the planned fifty-four million pounds Millennium Project … the International Centre for Life.

This 1906 photograph is included by kind permission of Tyne and Wear Development Corporation.

The building (now the property of Northumbria University) is built of red brick, which was unusual for John Dobson, who normally worked in stone. However, the windows are of stone.

The lay-out of the windows is rather unusual; symmetrical in pattern and all recessed – tall, arched windows above smaller ones below and all below a pediment.

The Newcastle Daily Journal of January 16th, 1865, simply described the school as 'classical'.

It is believed the Riding School was built, for the Northumberland Yeomanry, in 1847.

A colourful and detailed, contemporary account of the Arcade was published in the Newcastle Daily Journal, on may 19th, 1832: it reads – "This magnificent building, now the scaffolding in front is removed, and the various works approach to a completion, has excited the liveliest emotions of pleasure in the minds of the inhabitants of Newcastle, and the admiration of every stranger.

From its situation, the magnitude, the splendour of the front, the beauty of the interior – with the long row of conical windows in the roof, throwing a rich stream of light upon the chequered marble pavement beneath – and the excellence of its arrangement throughout, the Royal Arcade cannot fail to become a prominent ornament to the town and an object of attraction to every intelligent visitor."

The account continues –

"Were we to omit all record of so spirited an undertaking we should neglect a portion of our duty, and we have therefore been at some pains to collect the following particulars, which we have pleasure in laying before our readers.

The front, adjoining Pilgrim Street and facing Mosley Street, is of elegant polished stone, ninety-four feet wide and seventy-five feet high. The architecture of the basement storey is of the Doric order, with an enriched entablature surmounted with six fluted, Corinthian columns. On the attic is a beautifully turned balustrade, also of stone, in front of which, in the centre of the building, is to be placed a group of five figures, 'Britannica' being the most prominent."

"The rooms on the north side of the entrance will, we learn, be occupied as the banking home of Messrs. Backhouse and Co, and those on the south side as the Savings Bank, over which will be three large, public rooms. The interior of the Arcade is 250 feet long, 20 feet wide and 35 feet high, having conical, ornamental skylights raised upon an arched, groined ceiling richly furnished with pure Grecian ornament.

On each side of the Arcade are eight large and elegant shops, the first and second storeys having been arranged with very convenience for offices. At the east end of the Arcade are a suite and spending apartments comprising a News Room, Auction Mart and a room for public purpose (72 feet by 32 feet), with ante-rooms adjoining. Above, there is to be a conservatory with Medical Vapour and warm and cold baths adjoining. Underneath the whole of the spending line of buildings are large arched vaults with offices, the entrance to which are Manor Chare. Some idea may be found of the great skill, assiduity and judgement by which the various operators have been directed by Mr Grainger, when we state that although all the apartments, offices, shops and public rooms are expected to be fully occupied in the course of a few weeks, it is not yet twelve months since the first stone was laid. The munificent spirit by which so great a public ornament has been directed, and so much public accommodation provided, will not go unappreciated."

If only this glowing and enthusiastic testimonial had been corroborated by unfolding events – but, alas, it was not to be. The sad history of the Arcade is well documented and a number of books, still available, by local authors, contain fulsome and colourful accounts of its demise.

From designs by John Dobson, work had begun on the site of the present-day Swan House, at the bottom of Pilgrim Street, in June 1831 and, remarkably, was completed just short of a year later, in May 1832. This was a shopping arcade the like of which Newcastle had never seen before, even though it was not uncommon in the fashionable capitals of London and Paris. It was, without doubt, a major contribution to the town's public architecture and was closely based, so it was said, on the highly successful and prestigious Lowther Arcade, in London; yet, it was deemed to b (particularly in the manner of its lighting) superior to the London arcade and thus was recognised as being the finest in the country.

It cost almost £45,000 to build it. It housed not only shops but also offices and other amenities all listed in the Daily Journal's account. The interior was floored with chequered stone and black marble and it was lit by eight conical skylights set in domes in the roof. Its architectural attractions were both manifold and marvellous. Unfortunately, however, despite its impressive appearance and the many attractions mentioned Richard Grainger, the builder of the Arcade had neglected to give proper thought and consideration to its sighting – an oversight which was to have disastrous consequences.

271

In fact, the Arcade experienced commercial difficulties, as a result of its unpopular location, right from the very beginning and it was therefore never the commercial success it was confidently expected to be.

The Royal Arcade was described by Faulkner and Greg as "one of John Dobson's most dignified compositions".

The present (2008) interior of 'the Arcade' is Bar 55°, part of the Swan House and still situated at the very bottom of Pilgrim Street.

The Daily Journal's correspondent had boldly forecast that "all the apartments, offices and shops… are expected to be fully occupied in the course of a few weeks…", yet by 1841 (nine years later!) some of these same stops had still not been let. The Post Office, vacated its premises in the 1860s and gradually, one after another, the offices emptied until by the end of the century they were almost exclusively occupied by "furniture brokers and second-hand dealers".

Demolition of the entire Arcade was seriously proposed as early as the 1880s. Having been left to gradually decay for several decades (- it was described by N Tarn, in the Northern Architect, of March 1963, as "an embarrassing white elephant") it was finally demolished in 1963. During demolition each stone was carefully numbered and stored with the intention of rebuilding the Arcade elsewhere – but it never happened! A replica (in fibre glass!) of the interior of John Dobson's magnificent original Royal Arcade was constructed at a later date. Situated beneath Swan House – ironically and arguably the ugliest building in the whole of Newcastle: this 'fake' cost more to build than the elegant original.

The fact that the Royal Arcade was a commercial failure, practically from the outset, was due entirely to the unusually bad judgement shown by Richard Grainger, the man who, probably more than any other, was responsible for bringing so many wonderful buildings to the town and city of Newcastle.

Quite simply, he built the Arcade in the "wrong" part of the town or, as The Penny Magazine so aptly and succinctly put it "… he (Grainger) failed in this one instance to take sufficient notice of both topography and trend".

The Royal Station Hotel   (Neville Street)

John Dobson's hotel of c.1835 is now less than one quarter of the present building: the section west of the main entrance, closest to the station, is Dobson's original hotel, though in 1890 a further three floors were added to the four-storey, ten-bays that were the original building. Dobson's hotel had reception rooms on the ground floor, grand suites with high ceilings on the first floor and smaller rooms above: one hundred bedrooms in total "for families and single people". The first floor windows have architraves and pediments.

St Mary's Place   (Newcastle upon Tyne)

Described as an ashlar-fronted terrace in Tudor style and built in 1829-30 to designs by John Dobson "to complement his Church of St Thomas the Martyr, opposite.

The majority of ground floor frontages have given way to rather gaudy, incongruous 'shop fronts'.

Fortunately, however, a few of the originals still exist: *Midland Bank (now HSBC, 2008), for example, has preserved the original doorway with its flight of stone steps, flanked by iron railings.

274

St Mary's Place, Newcastle upon Tyne (top and bottom).

Archaelogia Aeliana, vol XIII, gives us the following information – The seventeenth century houses (the property of Trinity House) on the south side of the Chapel on Broad Chare, had been frequently repaired and altered, so much so that, by the early nineteenth century, it had been decided to rebuild two of them.

On the third of May, 1841 John Dobson (the advising architect) attended a meeting of 'the Board (of Trinity House), where he gave his estimate (the sum of £257-15-03) for the dismantling of the remains of the two warehouses and rebuilding them completely, a proposal which was agreed by the Board.

The entrance from Broad Chare.

This work was carried out during 1841. The builder was Richard Cail and his joiner was one Mr McAllister.

John Dobson duly presented the tradesmen's bills for payment as each stage of the work was completed. The final bill was paid on December 6th, 1841 to a Mr Oliver (Architect) – though whether this was Andrew or Thomas Oliver isn't known"… for drawing plans of the warehouse in Broad Chare".

John Dobson, it is claimed, renewed the old doorway and the three cellar windows on the north side of the passage leading from Broad Chare.

Although for many years, John Dobson was entered in Trinity House's books as their architect, his contribution appears to have been largely consultative. The system seems to have been that his office prepared drawings for minor alterations only – his role in the rebuilding of the two warehouses, for example, was that of adviser and intermediary, notwithstanding the advertisement (in the Newcastle Daily Chronicle of Saturday, April 3rd, 1841), inviting builders to tender for the work, which said: "Plans of the Buildings and specifications of the various works to be seen at Mr Dobson's office, in Newcastle".

In the main courtyard are the Almshouses of 1787.

The mock-Tudor façade of the building on Broad Chare, of 1841, hides the secluded courtyard. The south side was built in 1721. Beyond it is a smaller courtyard and the school, which still has a library of some three thousand books. The entrance hall was rebuilt in 1800 and measures roughly twenty feet by eighteen.

From its beginning Trinity House was a religious institution. The interior fittings of the present chapel were erected in 1634: repairs to the walls were carried out in 1651 and 1794. The windows in the south and east sides belong to this latter date. The Chapel is still used by the Brethren once a year. The Banqueting Hall was built in 1721: it is a spacious and beautiful room panelled in mahogany with many fine pictures on the walls. The Board Room is also large with many old prints on display.

Behind the Hall is the smaller; courtyard and the School of 1753, with its collection of more than three thousand books.

"To step into Trinity House courtyard (top) is like straying into a different calmer age … it is the peace, the feeling of oasis, that most impresses".
(David Bean),

The Chapel (left), is on the east side, received its staircase and Tuscan porch in 1800, but it was remodelled in 1841. The Chapel is still used by the Brethren once a year.

The Watergate Building stands on the site of the old Bridge Chapel of St Thomas the Martyr, which was demolished in 1830 "because it obstructed traffic". The present building, which took its place, was designed by John Dobson and has the 'same classical features and proportions' as Grainger's fine buildings further north in the town. It was extended east, in the same style, later in the century.

281

John Dobson's grave (with marble headstone) in the cemetery he designed.

Dobson's passing was not felt to mark the end of an era in Newcastle nor was it felt in the profound way in which (Richard) Grainger's was. So much of Dobson's work had been spread throughout Northumberland and Durham… on the designing of country homes.

Dobson had always been a quiet and retiring professional man and had never become (and would have hated to become) the ebullient public figure which Grainger had been (Tyneside Classical).

It speaks volumes for the 'area of is birth', however that the site of his birth in Chirton, North Shields is a public house (now thankfully restored), which for some long time was boarded up and covered in graffiti, and which boasts a small plaque above the entrance stating he died in 1867; his house on New Bridge Street became a lodging house, then part of a dance-hall and is now a nightclub; his resting place in Jesmond Cemetery (above) was (when this picture was taken) closely overgrown with nettles and briars – and a memorial to both his memory and his genius, more singularly inappropriate than one could possibly imagine, is that the city street which bears his name should be one of the ugliest in the whole of Newcastle.

Tributes

John Dobson died at nine o'clock in the morning of January 8th, 1865, at his house on New Bridge Street, Newcastle.

His funeral took place on Saturday, January 14th, when his earthly remains were interred, alongside those of his late wife, Isabella (who had died on February 13th, 1846, aged fifty-one years), at the Newcastle General Cemetery in Jesmond.

"The ceremony was not attended by such large numbers of the public as might have witnessed the burial of the greatest architect of the North of England… ", wrote the Newcastle Daily Journal (January 14th, 1865) which, if taken out of context, might give a totally erroneous impression and be surprising in the extreme, considering the popularity of the deceased and the high esteem in which John Dobson was held. However, the newspaper explained in its report that, "the relatives of the deceased were anxious for as much privacy as possible…" While to a large extent the family's wishes were complied with his fellow townsmen were understandably disappointed at being deprived the opportunity to pay their final respects to a man of "private worth and great professional reputation".

Thus the life of this extraordinary character came to an end, and many indeed there were who mourned his passing, for it is so often the case that a man's life and work are not truly appreciated until he is dead – and history is littered with examples to support this point of view: not so with John Dobson.

This was a man whose creative genius was widely recognised not only after his passing but happily during the many years of his prodigious working life, by friends, colleagues, employers and employees alike.

Space, unfortunately, does not permit me to list the very many tributes paid to this 'architectural colossus', by writers who have carefully studied and examined John Dobson's work, but it is both appropriate and illuminating, nevertheless, to record some, at least, of their acknowledgements.

The Newcastle Daily Journal, writing shortly after his death, had this to say:

"….there are few buildings of any note n this town or in Northumberland, with which his name is not in some way associated". "… the versatility of his talent is shown by the erection of buildings from his designs, adapted for almost every purpose".

A week or so later this same newspaper concluded:

"…it may be questioned whether any architect, in London or the provinces, has ever designed and carried out such a number of buildings and of such miscellaneous character. Mr Dobson's genius was not confined to any one particular branch of architecture; but whatever description of buildings he had to erect his ability was displayed both in its design, to mark its purpose, and in adapting its internal arrangements most effectively for its requirements".

Tom Faulkner and Andrew Greg (John Dobson, Newcastle Architect, 1787-1865) paid several complimentary references to Dobson's abilities and character:

"A man who contributed more than any other to the architecture of the North-East and Tyneside in particular. Dobson brought to the region London's most fashionable ideas together with a Geordie's down-to-earth practicality."

Photograph included by kind permission of Macdonald Hotels: Julia C Marshall, Manager; Linden Hall Hotel, Longhorsley, Northumberland

Faulkner and Greg make the following observations:
"Immensely versatile in the range and styles of his buildings; he designed fine houses for the local gentry, noble crescents and squares for the middle classes, hotels and railway stations for travellers, and churches, schools, hospitals, baths and prisons for everyone. He was an immensely respected and important provincial architect of considerable national renown."

Lyall Wilkes is another who respected and admired both John Dobson's work and the man himself. In a postscript to his book, John Dobson, Architect and Landscape Gardener, Wilkes made the following astute observation: "Nothing reflects the spirit of the age more truthfully that its architecture, except, perhaps, its coinage, which also cannot hide debasement. Visiting a great country house by Dobson and seeing the confidence and wealth and belief in the future of which it is an expression, one is compelled to realise that its spirit is as alien to our present age as are the Pyramids...."

The Builder (January 14th, 1865) paid him the two following compliments, mentioning "the versatility of Mr Dobson's talent in turning his hand to work of any kind...": "The timber framework used as staithes for shipping coals on the Tyne shows that Mr Dobson was a master of carpentry; the graving-dock, designed for Messrs Smith, at St Peter's shipyard, proved him an engineer; and the warehouse built at the docks at Sunderland and Jarrow, showed that the massive construction came as easily to his hand as the Gothic churches or luxurious mansions."

In its second tribute The Builder simply said, "A history of Mr Dobson's works would be the history of nearly every territorial residence in the County (of Northumberland)."

Nikolaus Pevsner adds his contribution with the comment: "It was due to Dobson (and Grainger) that the centre of Newcastle became a composition in the best possible taste – well planned, well built and well designed." And of Dobson's country houses he adds: "… noble designs which establish him at once as one of the best amongst the architects of his generation in England."

Finally, though this is only a small sample of the many tributes paid him, John Grundie and Grace McCombie described Dobson as:- "The most prominent and most talented of the group of the pantheon of local (ie Tyneside) architects who emerged in the early part of the nineteenth century... among the best architects of his generation in the whole of England".

But it was not just his architectural skills that evoked sincere admiration; it was the nature and character of the man himself. The Builder refers to his "upright conduct as a man and his generous and kindly nature."

The Newcastle Weekly Chronicle (January 1st, 1887) described him as: "… a man of genial temper, generous, modest, simple, unassuming, warm-hearted and honourable."

These are all glowing and richly deserved tributes, indicative of the esteem and affection in which John Dobson was rightly held by both is contemporaries and those who, since, have written about his work. But perhaps it is fitting that the final words (a tribute to his character rather than the fine quality of his workmanship) should be left to his daughter, Margaret Jane, who in her Memoir of 1885 wrote: "He never exceeded an estimate and never had a legal dispute with a contractor."

Bibliography

Margaret Jane Dobson, *A Memoir of John Dobson*, Lambert and Co., Newcastle, 1885

Tom Faulkner and Andrew Greg, *John Dobson, Newcastle Architect, 1787-1865,* Tyne and Wear Museums Service, 1987

Niklaus Pevsner, the *Buildings of England; Northumberland*, Penguin, 1957

Pevsner and Richmond, *The Buildings of England; Northumberland*, Penguin, 1992

W W Tomlinson, *Comprehensive Guide to Northumberland*, W H Robinson, 11th edition

Lyall Wilkes, *John Dobson, Architect and Landscape Gardener*, Oriel Press, 1980

Bruce Allsopp and Ursula Clark, *Historic Architecture of Northumberland and Newcastle upon Tyne*, Oriel Press, 1977

Stanley Prins and Roger Massingberd-Mundy ed., *A Guide to the Anglican Churches in Newcastle and Northumberland*, Newcastle Diocesan Bishop's Editorial Committee of THE LINK, 1982

Frank Graham, *The Old Halls, Houses and Inns of Northumberland*, 1977

Frank Graham, *Tynedale from Blanchland to Carter Bar*, 1978

Robert Hugill, *Castle and Peles of the English Border,* Frank Graham, 1970

Lyall Wilkes and Gordon Dodds, *Tyneside Classical*, John Murray, 1964

Lyall Wilkes, *Tyneside Portraits*, Frank Graham, 1971

Pevsner and Williamson, *The Building of England; County Durham*, Penguin, 1983

The Rev J Hodgson and Mr F C Laird, *The Beauties of England and Wales*, vol. 12, pt 1, Northumberland and Nottinghamshire, 1813

Tyne and Wear County Council Museums, *The Tyneside Classical Tradition; Classical Architecture in the North-East, c.1700-1850*, published to accompany the Exhibition held in the Laing Art Gallery, Newcastle upon Tyne, 15th July – 17th August, 1980

David Bean, *Newcastle 900: A Portrait of Newcastle upon Tyne*, Newcastle upon Tyne City Council for Newcastle, 900, 1980

Peter Winter and David Milne, Jonathan Brown, Alan Rushworth, *Newcastle upon Tyne*, Northern Heritage Consultancy Ltd, 1989.

T H Rowland, *Waters of Tyne*, T H Rowland, 1991

T H Rowland, *Discovering Northumberland*, Frank Graham 1973

Thomas Faulkner and Phoebe Lowery, *Lost Houses of Newcastle and Northumberland*, Jill Raines, 1996

David Crystal, *Cambridge Biographical Encyclopaedia*, Cambridge University Press, 1995

P Anderson Graham, *Highways and Byways in Northumbria*, MacMillan and Co, 1920

Neville Whittaker, *The Old Halls and Manor Houses of Durham*, Frank Graham, 1975

Frank Graham, *Newcastle upon Tyne; Sixty Views from Old Prints and Original Drawings*, Frank Graham, 1984

Arthur Mee, *The King's England: Northumberland*, C L S Linnell, revised and ed,, Hodder and Stoughtonn, 1964

Frank Atkinson, *Victorian Britain: The North East*, David and Charles, 1989

Sydney Middlebrook, *Newcastle upon Tyne: Its Growth and Achievements*, S R Publishers Ltd, reprint, 1968

H L Honeyman, *Northumberland*, County Books series, Robert Hale Ltd, 1949

M J Jackson, *Castles of Northumbria*, Barmkin Books, 1992

Mike Kirkup, *Was There Ever a Railway Row? A History of North Seaton Colliery and Village,* Woodhorn Press, 1997

George MacDonald Fraser, *The Steel Bonnets*, Pan Books, 1974

Peter Meadows and Edward Waterson, *Lost Houses of County Durham*, Jill Raines, 1993

Neville Whittaker and Ursula Clark, *Historic Architecture of County Durham*, Oriel Press, 1971

William Parsons and William White, H*istory, Directory and Gazetteer of Durham and Northumberland*, vols. 1 & 2, Edward Baines and Son, Leeds Mercury Office, 1827 and 1828

F W Manders, *History of Gateshead*, 1973

Department of the Environment, *An Historical, Topographical and Descriptive View of the County Palatine of Durham*, vol. 1, Mackenzie and Ross, 1834

Department of the Environment, *A List of Buildings of Special Architectural or Historic Interest: District of Gateshead,* Department of the Environment, 1987

Department of the Environment, *A List of Buildings of Special Architectural or Historic Interest: District of Newcastle, Tyne and Wear,* Department of the Environment, 1987

Howard Colvin, *A Biographical Dictionary of British Architects, 1600-1840*, John Murray, 1978

Anon, Ward's *Dictionary for Newcastle, including Gateshead, Shields and Sunderland*, R Ward and Sons, 1915-16

Robert Hugill, *Castles of Durham*, Frank Graham, 1979

G M Trevelyan, *Grey of Fallodon*, Longmans Green and Co, 1937

Frank Graham, *The Bridges of Northumberland and Durham*, Frank Graham, 1975

John Hodgson, *A History of Morpeth* (Frank Graham's facsimile edition of Hodgson's original 1832 publication), 1973

A H Tweddle, *Town Trail for Morpethians* (series), A H Tweddle, 1984

Eva James, *A History of St Nicholas' Church, Cramlington*, E James n.d.

Oswin Craster, *A History of Embleton Parish Church* (Photography by George Skipper, Designed by Sue Dale), n.d.

David Lovie, *The Buildings of Grainger Town: Four Townscape Walks around Newcastle,* English Partnerships, 1997

P R B Brooks, *Wylam, A History in Photographs*, Northumberland County Library, 1995

Anon, *The Newcastle Daily Journal*, various editions

Anon, *The Newcastle Daily Chronicle*, various editions

Anon, *The Newcastle Courant*, various editions

Anon, *The Tyne Mercury*, various editions

*The following books were used by Miss Carol Ward in her thesis on The Leazes, Hexham, which she very graciously allowed me to borrow and make extensive use of:-

Andrew Jackson Downing, *The Architecture of Country Houses, 1816-52*, Da Capo, 1968

Mark Girouard, *Life in the English Country House*, Yale University Press, 1978

Jill Franklin, *The Gentleman's Country House, 1835-1914*, Routledge and Kegan Paul, 1981

Martin Page, *Historic Houses Restored and Preserved*, Whitney Library of Design, 1979